Franz Hettinger, Henry Sebastian Bowden

Revealed Religion

Franz Hettinger, Henry Sebastian Bowden

Revealed Religion

ISBN/EAN: 9783743383531

Manufactured in Europe, USA, Canada, Australia, Japa

Cover: Foto ©Lupo / pixelio.de

Manufactured and distributed by brebook publishing software (www.brebook.com)

Franz Hettinger, Henry Sebastian Bowden

Revealed Religion

REVEALED RELIGION

FROM THE "APOLOGIE DES CHRISTENTHUMS"

OF

FRANZ HETTINGER, D.D.
PROFESSOR OF THEOLOGY AT THE UNIVERSITY
OF WURZBURG

EDITED

WITH AN INTRODUCTION ON THE ASSENT OF FAITH

BY

HENRY SEBASTIAN BOWDEN
OF THE ORATORY

FR. PUSTET & CO.
NEW YORK AND CINCINNATI

PREFACE

THE claims of Christianity are to be tested, according to the modern scientific method, like those of any human Creed. Its origin must be sought in the ideas, political, philosophical, religious, current at its birth, and their influence on the mind of its Founder. Its moral worth will be determined by its agreement with the conclusions of reason, and its power of satisfying the higher needs of mankind. Thus, religion is treated like a philosophy or a language, as merely the product of human thought, and the notion of Revelation is set aside. Now Reason may indeed reject a creed as worthless, if its doctrines, though professedly revealed, are manifestly absurd or licentious, as are those of Mahomedanism. But where the morality is undoubtedly pure, as is the case with Christianity, the only logical mode of inquiry is to examine, not the nature of the doctrines, in themselves professedly incomprehensible, but the external evidence for the fact that those doctrines are a revelation from God. Such is the method pursued by the earlier Christian apologists, and adopted in the present volume.

Revelation necessarily presupposes the truth of God's

existence. The evidence, therefore, for this fundamental doctrine formed the subject of the first volume of Dr. Hettinger's work, of which the English version, entitled "Natural Religion," was published in 1892, and is now in its second edition. As natural religion is founded on reason, so is revealed religion on faith; and since this term is variously understood, a preliminary introduction on its precise theological sense, the nature and motive of the assent required, has been prefixed by the Editor to the present volume. The treatise itself begins by showing that a revelation is neither impossible in itself, nor incompatible with the attributes of God already established, especially His immutability; and again, that such a communication is naturally desired by man. Though the rationalists assert that the perfectibility of the human race is to be attained by merely natural evolution, unaided by grace, a consideration of the heathen world, and of the failure of its best philosophers to overcome its idolatry and superstition, prove further that a revelation is a moral necessity for fallen man.

A revelation, however, could never claim acceptance unless it showed external signs of its authenticity, and this evidence is found in the visible, supernatural facts of miracle and prophecies. The characteristics of such phenomena have then to be fully considered, and their possibility demonstrated from the existence of an omnipotent Creator. Now comes the turning-point of the whole inquiry. Have these facts ever occurred, or, in other words, are the Gospels credible?

And it is shown that the narrative of the Evangelists, with all its miraculous details of the life of Christ, is an accurate and historical account of facts which really occurred, that it is supported by the contemporary evidence of trustworthy witnesses, both Latin, Greek, and Hebrew; and that the foundation of Christianity is inexplicable if the truth of the Gospels be rejected. As this evidence has been the special object of rationalistic attack, a critique by the Rev. H. Cator, of the Oratory, London, has been added in an Appendix, giving a summary of the theory of the Tübingen School as to the formation of the Christian Gospels, with a brief account of its value, and of the evidence for and against the whole hypothesis.

But, again, as regards miracles, Saints in all times have worked them; what was then peculiar to Christ's? The Saints wrought miracles in the power of God, and to approve themselves His messengers; Christ worked miracles in His own power, and to attest His own Divinity; and the last miracle of His earthly life, His Resurrection, was the crowning proof of His claim to be the Son of God. Hence the miracles of Christ, and especially His Resurrection, require to be examined from this point of view. For the same reason, the proof from prophecy has to be separately considered, for the fulfilment of prophecy in Christ furnishes even stronger evidence than the miracles that He alone was the Messias, the God-man foretold. And, again, the accomplishment in His Church of the predictions which He Himself made of His future Kingdom, testifies to His Divinity with increasing force, as each successive age witnesses their fulfilment.

As the rationalists profess to explain the rise and spread of Christianity by merely human causes, the inquiry fitly closes with an examination of these professed origins, and a brief consideration of the two systems, Mahomedan and Buddhist, which are commonly put forward as successful rivals of the religion of Christ.

The leading objections against Christianity have been the same in all time, and Dr. Hettinger, in dealing with them, naturally takes the Fathers and Schoolmen for his guides. These objections fall always under two chief heads. The rationalists, like the Jews, deny the fact of Revelation, the sceptics, like the Gentiles, its possibility. And neither Paulus or the older rationalists, or Strauss, or Renan, or any of the more modern type, have added substantially to the *a priori* arguments of Trypho and Celsus. In fact, the two former explain the Resurrection in the very words of Celsus, as the mere invention of a deluded woman. To a whole class of sceptical explanations of a similar kind the words of Origen fitly apply, "that the incredible character of such assertions palpably betray their falsehood."[1] Yet they pass current. The letters of the Mahatmas find evidence where the Epistles of St. Paul are rejected;

[1] *Celsus* i. 32.

and the ready acceptance, now so common, of any conjecture, however uncritical, wild, or irrational, provided it be only anti-Christian, is a fresh proof, if proof were needed, of the puerile credulity which is the nemesis of unbelief.

This holds good also of the "scientific" explanation of the formation of the Christian Gospels. According to Baur, the Gospels were forged, late in the second century, to effect and cement, under the apparent cloak of Apostolic authority, the reconciliation of the two rival parties of Peter and Paul, which till then had divided the Christian Body. Now, on what evidence does this statement rest? A pure assumption, contradicted by a successive chain of witnesses from Clement to Irenæus: this, we think, the Appendix clearly shows. But just as one Scriptural text, divorced from its surroundings, and with a forced meaning, has been made the basis of each successive heresy, from Arius to Luther, so it is with Baur. A solitary and eccentric writer, an apocryphal Gospel, a pronounced heresiarch are to silence the voice of all the recognised authorities of the Church, and the joint-witness of Africa and Italy, of Gaul and Palestine. And so far from any true advance in Biblical learning being on the side of the sceptics, the new matter brought to light in this century, such as Tatian's *Diatessaron*, the "Apology" of Aristides, and the Epitaph of St. Abercius, corroborate, directly or indirectly, the traditional authority of the Gospels, and the unbroken, continuous unity of the Christian Church.

One instance will suffice to show how new documents are treated by the scientists if they present facts adverse to their theory. The *Diatessaron*, by its very name, showed the supreme and exclusive authority enjoyed by Gospels, four in number, at the time of its composition, about A.D. 150, or within fifty years of the date of St. John's Gospel. What, then, were these four? "Not the Canonical Gospels," says the author of "Supernatural Religion," "some other four, that of the Hebrews, or of Peter amongst others," or "the *Diatessaron* seems never to have been seen, probably for the simple reason that there was no such work." Thus spoke the oracle in 1875. In 1888, however, an Arabic version of the *Diatessaron* is brought to light from the Vatican Library by Father Ciasca, and published with his Latin translation of the same work. The Arabic version is allowed by all critics accurately to represent the original, and is found to contain the four Gospels, including St. John's, in their entirety, with the exception of the Genealogies. What, then, says our advanced critic? Without any apology for the groundlessness of his previous assertion, and with a happy contempt for facts and evidence, he finds traces, invisible to others, of an apocryphal Gospel, the Pseudo-Peter, in the work before him, and declares that it ought to have been called the *Diapente*.[1] Thus, now that the document declared by him as

---

[1] Cf. *The Diatessaron of Tatian*, by Rev. M. Maher, S.J. Catholic Truth Society.

probably non-existent is discovered, he asserts that it is not what it calls itself, and that he knows more about it than the author himself, and this audacity succeeds, not indeed with any competent judge, but with the public at large. Like the twice slain hero of a melodrama, our critic returns sound and scatheless at the end of the piece to receive the popular applause.

While care has been taken that the leading sceptical arguments should be fully, and as it is believed, fairly considered, it must always be remembered that no defence of Christianity can, or need, discuss the multitude of hypotheses which are ever in process of production. They are ephemeral, they appear and die of themselves almost in the hour of their birth, and in many cases they are mutually destructive. Since 1850 there have been published 747 theories regarding the Old and New Testament, of which 608 are now defunct.[1] The aim of the present volume, then, has been to bring clearly to the front the leading principles of Christianity and scepticism, as the most valid and effective method of inquiry into the whole subject, and of elucidating the truth.

The traditional methods of defence, pursued in the following pages, will, of course, find little favour with those who look for an apology of Christianity impregnated in every line by "Zeitgeist," and couched in the terms of Post-Kantian philosophy. Two reasons may be adduced for the adhering to the older, and, as

[1] *Higher Criticism*, H. L. Hastings, Anti-infidel Library.

some would consider, exploded method. First, then, the new school of apologists have not produced encouraging results. Its more conspicuous writers, though by no means deficient in ability, research, or zeal, have, again and again, committed themselves to untenable propositions, and have, not unfrequently, incurred the condemnation of the Church. Whence, then, has this failure arisen?

They entered on their work with two principles assumed as certain: first, that scholastic theology was no longer a serviceable weapon; and secondly, that it was their task to recast Catholic truth in one or other form of modern thought. Thus it was that Gunther attempted to Catholicise the teaching of Hegel, Hermes, that of Kant, Froschammer, the historical canons of criticism of the Munich School, Bautain, and Bonetty, the principle of traditionalism, Rosmini, and, to a certain extent, Gratry, the ontological theories then popular; the result in each case being the production of hybrid doctrines, which were alike condemned by the Church, and rejected by the non-Catholic schools, which they were intended to conciliate. Nor is the reason far to find. The avowed contempt of these writers for theology proper led them to disregard its study, and they thus wrote with but a superficial knowledge of the very doctrines they professed to defend, while at the same time their admiration for non-Catholic systems blinded them to the fundamental errors on which these systems were based.

Now, the strictest scholastic theologian must admit

that the scientific defence of Christian doctrine, like everything finite, admits of improvement; that different times require different treatment. Bossuet's "Variations," for instance, are inapplicable to the modern Anglican. Lastly, that every true advance in knowledge must, as far as it bears on the subject, be turned to account, as Leo XIII. has laid down, especially with regard to Biblical studies. But it must also be remembered that, while the Church may change the form of her defence, as St. Peter used one set of arguments with the Jews, and St. Paul another with the Gentiles, her doctrines themselves are necessarily and always immutable. As she did not create the faith, neither can she change it. She teaches what she has heard; she ordains what she has been told. She cannot modify one doctrine—say that of eternal punishment—or tamper with the exactness of its expression, even though by doing so she would win half the world. Her mission is to convert the nations to the truth, not to adapt the truth to them; and every attempt to do so must be fatal alike to the cause of truth and to the souls it is designed to serve. Secondly, amidst the various systems available for the exposition or defence of Catholic truth, one, and one only, has been specially commended by the Church in the past as in the present—the scholastic method, and, above all, the teaching of St. Thomas. The Summa is far more than Aristotle Christianised. It is the whole circle of revealed truth defined, defended, and illustrated; and the marvellous penetration, grasp, and accuracy of the angelic doctor are attested by the many cases in which his conclusions have anticipated doctrinal decisions and refuted future heresies. For six centuries it has held a place absolutely unrivalled in the councils of the Church, and in her theological schools. While on the other hand, "ever since its rise," says Melchior Canus, "contempt of scholasticism, and the pest of heresies have gone hand in hand." Wicliff, Luther, Melancthon, the Jansenists, each in turn reviled the schoolmen, as do now the admirers of Hegel or Kant; and the reason of this diametrical opposition between Scholasticism and non-Catholic systems is, that while the former is based on the objective reality of our sense and intellectual knowledge, the latter, as a rule, depend wholly on the subjective consciousness of the individual ego, wherein certainty is never attained. And, since theology presupposes the physical reality of the external world, as in its proof of God's existence from His visible creation, and its definition of the Real Presence under the actually extended species of the Holy Eucharist, Scholasticism becomes its natural "handmaid;" while no system of subjective idealism can be made to harmonise with Christian dogmas, or serve as a vehicle of revealed truth.

In the present version, Chapter XII., "Der Weg des vernünftigen Glaubens," has been omitted, as its main arguments are given in the Introduction by the Editor on the "Assent of Faith." Chapter XVII., " Christi Wort und Werk," and Chapter XVIII., "Die Person Jesu Christi," have been summarised and recast under the title of "Christ and Christianity." The chapters have been numbered *ab initio*, and not as a sequence of Volume I. Thus Chapter X. of the original is Chapter I. of " Revealed Religion." The title of this chapter has also been changed from " Glaube und Geheimniss" to "The Possibility of Revelation." The original German has been considerably curtailed and reset, and the footnotes have been incorporated in the text. An Appendix by the Rev. H. Cator, on " The Tübingen Theory," as has been said, has been added to the present version. In conclusion, the Editor desires to express his indebtedness to the Rev. W. Gildea, D.D., for his valuable censorship of this version.

TABLE OF CONTENTS

INTRODUCTION

THE ASSENT OF FAITH

	PAGE
Definition of Faith. Kant, Hegel, *Lux Mundi*	1
Pietists make Faith a purely subjective assent	2
The motive of Catholic Faith objective	3
Belief on the authority of God speaking	4
Faith a supernatural virtue, impossible without grace	5
Non-Catholic proofs of a Revelation only intrinsic	6
Protestants, the Bible only	7
Rationalists, the doctrines as approved by reason	7
Fichte's Pantheistic Christianity	8
Catholics prove Revelation from external evidence	9
As is shown from the Fathers	10
The twofold proof of miracles and prophecy	11
Interior evidence, negative and positive	12
Theology defends and defines doctrine	13
But interior evidence confirmatory, not demonstrative	14
Reality of the proof from miracles	15
The Gospels more credible than any secular history	16
Evidence and certitude contrasted	17
Revelation certain, not evident	18
Doubt possible if a maximum of proof be demanded	19
The precepts of faith and charity	20
The certainty of faith *super omnia*, subjective	21
Because of the homage of the will to God speaking	22
Co-operation of reason and grace	23
Faith, knowledge, vision	24

CHAPTER I

POSSIBILITY OF REVELATION

	PAGE
Natural knowledge of God insufficient	27
God illuminates the soul from within	28
Natural inspiration, Mozart	29
Universal belief in Revelation	30
God unchanged by revealing	31
Revelation attested by external signs	32
Faith without knowledge superstition	33
Knowledge without faith scepticism	34
Mysteries in nature	35
Agreement of reason and faith	36
Belief in mystery the beginning of a supernatural life	37
And the principle of all true religion	38
The light of faith explains sacred mysteries	39
And illuminates merely natural truths	40
Corruptions of heathenism	41
Triumphs of faith	42

CHAPTER II

NECESSITY OF REVELATION

Traditionalism by depreciating reason	44
Leaves no logical defence for religion	45
Fallen human nature, though wounded, still entire	46
Necessity of Revelation relative, not absolute	47
Religions of paganism superstitious and cruel	48
Human sacrifices	49
Contempt of pagans for their gods	50
Truth sought in vain	51
Idolatry maintained for state purposes	52
Scepticism and superstition naturally allied	53
Degrading beliefs and advanced civilisation	54
Heathen sages not teachers	55
Their errors and immoralities	56
Wisdom for the few	57

CONTENTS

	PAGE
Contempt of the multitude	58
Failure of reason unaided by grace	59
One teacher only, Christ and His Church	60
Teaches all men all truth	61
And its teaching forms the basis of morality	62
Christianity shows also the nature of sin	63
And for the sacrifices of paganism	64
Substitutes the one atonement in Christ	65
In Him all things are restored	66
In temptation and conflict	67
The Christian conquers through Christ	68

CHAPTER III

MIRACLES AND PROPHECY

Revelation an external fact, attested by miracles and prophecy	70
A miracle defined	71
Threefold division of miracles	72
Universal practice of prayer shows belief in possibility of miracles	73
This belief is reasonable, and in accordance with the order of God's Providence	74
The miraculous in nature	75
Twofold end of creatures, particular and universal	76
Miracles never denied by Jews or pagans	77
Distinguishing marks of true and false miracles	78
True miracles the seal on Divine truth	79
Objections to miracles	80
They imply no change in God	81
The moral necessity of miracles, as arresting the attention of all	82
And begetting conviction of the truths they attest	83
Modern depreciation of their value, sign of unbelief	84
Hume's objection	85
Rests on two gratuitous assumptions	86
A miracle cognisable with only ordinary knowledge	87
As is shown by several instances	88
Prophecy defined	89
Prophecies, like miracles, true and false	90
Oracles and mediums	91
Marks of a prophet from God	92
The sceptic's demand of a miracle unreal and unreasonable	93

CHAPTER IV

CREDIBILITY OF THE GOSPELS

	PAGE
External evidence of their credibility furnished	95
By the transformation of the world by Christianity	95
Which is inexplicable, unless the Gospel narrative be true	96
The independent witness of pagan historians	97
Tacitus—Suetonius	98
Official report on Christians of Pliny	99
Josephus	100
The Jewish Talmud	101
The Gospel a witness to its own truth	102
The Gospels as public documents	103
Texts and authorship jealously guarded	104
Patristic evidence to their number and rank	105
Down to close of second century	106
External evidence—The Itala, the Peschito, heretical writers	107
The Church's custody of apostolic tradition	108
And of unity of faith	109
Internal evidence—Their simplicity and directness	110
Competency of the Evangelists as biographers of Christ	111
The character they describe wholly original	112
Forgery impossible	113
Renan's inventions and conjectures	114
Gospel accuracy of detail	115
The records of eye-witnesses	116
Personal qualifications of the Evangelists	117
Special weight of St. Paul's evidence	118
The sceptical-mythical theory	119
If Christianity a popular myth, why then persecuted?	120
Why did it find expression in Christianity alone?	121
The myth, the product of a race in its infancy	122
The Gospel period an age of culture and criticism	123
The Gospels universally accepted 150 A.D.	124
The Gospel discrepancies a proof of their truth	125
Individual representations of one central Figure	126
Agreement of St. John and the Synoptics	127
Apocryphal and Canonical Gospels contrasted	128
Vitality of the Gospels	129

CONTENTS

CHAPTER V

THE DIVINITY OF CHRIST

	PAGE
Christ's appeal to His miracles	130
In proof of His Divinity	131
Connection of His words and works	132
Publicity of the miracles	133
Their symbolic character	134
Their effects clearly supernatural	135
Renan's attempted explanation	136
The subjects of His miraculous power	137
The sick and suffering	138
Self-sacrifice of Christ a moral miracle	139
The Resurrection the crowning miracle	140
Proofs of its reality	141
Change in the Apostles	142
Sceptical hypotheses, imaginary visions	143
Their evident improbability	144
Witness of St. Paul	145
The mythical theory	146
Sceptical objections ever the same	147
Conversion of the world without a miracle, itself miraculous	148

CHAPTER VI

PROPHECY AND FULFILMENT

Israel in itself insignificant	149
Yet most important as the Guardian of Revelation	150
Monotheism not "a Semitic instinct"	151
For Israel constantly relapses to idolatry	152
But a supernatural gift	153
Office of Israel to lead man to Christ	154
Universal expectation of the Messias, when Christ came	155
The priests and Herod, Zachary	156
Non-inspired writings, Josephus	157
Tacitus, Suetonius, Virgil	158
Inspired prophecy, patriarchs, Psalms	159

	PAGE
Twofold portraiture—glory and shame	160
The weeks of Daniel	161
The Minor Prophets	162
Fulfilment of prophecy in Christ	163
Cause of Israel's apostacy	164
Christ Himself a Prophet	165
The destruction of Jerusalem	166
Its attempted rebuilding	167
The Jews still a witness to Christ	168
Fulfilment of Christ's prophecies in His Church	169

CHAPTER VII

CHRIST AND CHRISTIANITY

Christianity always in conflict, whence its strength?	171
Alleged Christian origins	172
Yet those same causes failed in other systems	173
Christ, His words and works	174
His Passion and death	175
Christ and Socrates	176
Viator and Comprehensor	177
Power of His sacrifice	178
Christ reproduced in His followers	179
Rivals of Christianity	180
Mahomedanism merely naturalism	181
Buddhism essentially atheistic	182
The Church a standing miracle	183
Testimony of St. Cyprian	184

APPENDIX

THE TÜBINGEN THEORY

The date of the Gospels	187
General agreement of orthodox and rationalist critics	188
The difference as to authority and authorship	189
The so-called Petrine and Pauline parties	190
Evidence of St. Paul	191

CONTENTS

	PAGE
His relations with St. Peter	192
No sign of disunion in the Church	193
St. Ignatius and St. Polycarp	194
Hegesippus	195
Importance of his evidence for East and West	196
Justin Martyr and the Church of Ephesus	197
Irenæus, Gaul, and Asia Minor	198
His reverence for Rome	200
Continued chain of evidence	201
The Tübingen theory an arbitrary hypothesis	202
The Church one in Christ	203

INDEX . 205

INTRODUCTION

THE ASSENT OF FAITH[1]

THE term faith is taken in different senses by modern writers, their definitions being determined, as might be expected, by the principles concerning natural knowledge current in the schools of philosophy to which they belong.

Rationalists and followers of Kant, who deny the certainty of all objective knowledge, and regard the mind itself as the sole source of its cognition, understand by faith any undoubted assent which the mind forms for itself, such as its acceptance of a mathematical proof or of a fact of experience. Writers of the Hegelian and Pantheistic school, conformably with their theory that the object of knowledge is only and always the one absolute Being or substance, define faith as the means by which that substance, unseen in itself, is yet apprehended under phenomena, or is inferred as a cause from its effects or operations. Similarly with the ontologists, faith is nothing more than that process of reasoning, which discovers manifestations

[1] This introduction is based on the treatise on Faith by F. Kleutgen, S.J., *Theologie der Vorzeit*, V. iv.

A

of the divinity under the operations of nature, or, in a higher degree, in the life of Christ. So, too, with that phase of Anglicanism represented by "Lux mundi," Faith is a purely natural gift, which prompts our ventures for the unseen. It is the instinct of the relationship of the soul to God on our religious side, and the secret spring of new discoveries and of advance in science or commerce in secular life. The Pietistic or Evangelical school, never having been connected with any philosophical system, attempts no logical explanation of their theory, but affirms faith to be an inward assurance of salvation in the soul of the believer: a purely subjective conviction, devoid therefore of external proof. The untenableness of these theories will appear as we examine the Catholic definition of the term.

Faith differs from knowledge in that it is an assent determined, not by evidence, but by the authority of the informant. In its theological sense, faith is defined as "a supernatural virtue whereby we believe without doubt whatever God has revealed to man because He reveals it." The formal object or motive of faith is then, not the reasonableness of the doctrines taught, nor our apprehension of their truth, nor their adaptability to our needs, nor their sublime morality, but only and always the authority of God speaking, the subject-matter of faith being what He reveals. The formal object, though its importance is often unheeded, is essential to the assent of faith. As in the physical order the form determines things in their

ITS FORMAL MOTIVE

respective species, so with any science or virtue, it is the formal object which alone imparts to the subject-matter its specifically scientific or virtuous character. A mathematical proposition demonstrated by measurement, or by any principle not proper to the science, offers no mathematical proof. An action in itself charitable, almsgiving for instance, performed for vainglory or any motive not that of charity, would not be an act of that virtue. So also, an assent, even to the whole circle of revealed doctrine, formed on any other motive than that of God speaking, would not be an act of faith; the fact that He has spoken and His infallibility being related to the act of faith as the principles of a science are to the knowledge it includes, or the moral motive proper to a virtue is to the action by which it is exercised.

Let us now see how far the theological definition of faith is justified by the Gospels. Our Lord then claimed belief in His doctrine, not because it was His own, but as the word of His Father—God. "My doctrine is not Mine," He says, "but His who sent Me." And He repeatedly makes this appeal to His Father's authority.[1] So, too, with regard to the Apostles He says in His last prayer, "I have given them Thy word—Thy word is truth.[2] Thus possessed of the fact, the matter and infallibility of Revelation, the Apostles were sent forth to preach. They went as "ambassadors of Christ,"[3] and they demanded assent to their preaching, not as

[1] John v. 28, 30, 41; viii. 26. [2] John xvii. 8, 14.
[3] 2 Cor. v. 20; Eph. vi. 20.

the word of man, but "as it is indeed the Word of God that worketh in you that have believed."[1] And this message was incomprehensible. As divine truth, it was necessarily opposed to the false philosophies of man's invention; but, more than this, as a "mystery hidden in God," it was beyond the highest human wisdom. And yet this mystery was to bring into captivity every understanding, because the believer submitted his reason to Christ's Word on Christ's authority. Similarly St. John, after speaking of the power of faith in Christ to overcome the world, declares the divine testimony to be the source of its victories, and adds, "He that believeth in God hath the testimony of God in Himself, and he that believeth not the Son maketh Him (God) a liar."[2]

Faith, then, according to the New Testament, consists in an assent to what God says, because He says it. But neither the fact nor the infallibility of Revelation are so evident as to compel our assent. That assent is free, and the freedom of faith is its second important characteristic. The Scriptures again show this unmistakably, in that they everywhere set forth faith as a virtue, and declare the reward or punishment consequent on its exercise or neglect. Throughout the Old Testament the Jews are repeatedly reproached for the sin of their unbelief, while their rejection of the Messias and of the Revelation He brought was the cause of their final destruction. The moral value of faith arises from the important part exercised by the

[1] 1 Thess. ii. 13.   [2] 1 John v. 10.

will: first, in the disposition to believe—the "pius credulitatis affectus;" and secondly, in enjoining an assent "super omnia," proportioned, *not* to the evidence offered, but to the homage due to God speaking, the "obedience to the Gospel," as St. Paul calls it. The merit of this submission is declared in the plainest terms: "Without faith it is impossible to please God," and "By faith the just man lives."[1]

The reward of eternal life, promised repeatedly to faith, shows further that it is a supernatural virtue, and is therefore to be acquired by no merely human effort, but needs the help of grace. And this is so, not merely with regard to the assent itself, but also with regard to the very first inclination to believe. Yet the reason—apart from revelation—of this absolute necessity of grace is not at first sight apparent. Unprejudiced witnesses of our Lord's miracles must surely have had evidence sufficient, without supernatural aid, to produce conviction of their reality. The difficulty, again, of accepting mysteries which are beyond reason, and of submitting a corrupt will to external authority, is indeed great, but not insuperable. Formal heretics and apostates, who have culpably lost faith, and with it habitual grace, are as firmly attached to the errors of their sect as to what they still hold of truth. Grace, then, is absolutely necessary for faith, not in order to make the assent demanded, but because by faith we enter into a wholly supernatural order which leads to eternal life. The grace required is not "gratia medi-

[1] Heb. x. 38; xi. 6.

cinalis"—that is, the grace relatively necessary to heal the corruption of our fallen nature—but "gratia elevans," which is absolutely needed to make us heirs of Heaven. As, according to the divine plan, all creatures are naturally fitted to attain their end, and man, as an intellectual being, is endowed with reason, desire, and free-will for the pursuit of natural happiness, so also to reach his supernatural end he must be furnished with faculties corresponding thereto, that is, with the infused virtues of faith, hope, and charity. And since by faith alone we apprehend our higher end and the way thither, faith is the first of the supernatural virtues and the source and root of our justification.

Such, then, is faith in itself—belief on the authority of God speaking. But to believe on that authority certain other knowledge must be presupposed—the existence of God, the infallibility of His Word, and the fact that He has spoken. How, then, is this knowledge obtained?

The ultra-Protestant Biblical school, including Lutherans and Calvinists, hold, in accordance with their theory of faith, that the knowledge of God's existence and of His attributes, together with the fact that He has spoken, are all manifested to the believer by an immediate revelation conveyed through the Holy Scriptures. They condemn Catholics for appealing to logical proof or historic evidence; for the Word of God has power, they say, to prove itself divine. The same Spirit who speaks through its pages bears witness within us. There is no need, then, of grounds of faith, of instruction or reasoning, but only of experience. With this class may be ranked the false Mystics, Quietists, Anabaptists, and Quakers, who admit no external revelation, not even the Scriptures, but only the inward light, which, without any outward word or sign, the Spirit communicates to the unlearned and learned alike.

Rationalists agree with the Protestant school just described in holding that the doctrines of Christianity must be attested merely by their contents; but, instead of the inward spirit or light, they recognise reason alone as the supreme and sole arbiter in dogmatic as in other truth. The truth of Christianity is to be proved, therefore, not by external evidence of its divine origin, but solely by the agreement of its doctrines with the conceptions of reason and the moral needs of man. Such a system could only result in the elimination of the supernatural element in religion, as we see manifested in the *à priori* Biblical criticism now in vogue. Kant indeed openly declared, that if the Christian religion was not to do more harm than good, the Bible must be consigned to learned men, who, by expunging all the accretions of Jewish superstition in the way of mystery and miracle, may, although by a strained construction, reduce the doctrine of Jesus Christ to the religion and morals of pure reason.[1]

The Hegelian school, as represented by Schelling,

[1] *Religion innerhalb der Gränzen der reinen Vernunft*, 1794, 3. Stück, p. 152.

modified Kant's teaching, in so far as they professed to accept the mysteries of Christianity, which, however, they interpreted in a Pantheistic sense. The extent to which the most sacred doctrines were thus distorted and travestied may be seen from the following extracts from Fichte's "Way to a Blessed Life"[1]—"The intellectual vision," he says, "with which certain minds are endowed, apprehends God as the synthesis of all contradictions, and the only real Being in all things. Christ, therefore, being the first man who attained to this intelligence, is justly called 'the only Begotten and the Firstborn Son of God.' And though philosophy can of itself now discover this truth, yet it remains for ever certain that all who, since Christ, have arrived at this union with God, have done so only by His example, and therefore by Him alone. The regeneration of which He spoke means only the rising to this higher knowledge, and entering into this divine life. We arise from the grave at the voice of Christ when we emerge from the material conceptions of ordinary men, and realise what He taught. We eat His Flesh and Blood, and become Christs ourselves when we imitate His virtues; then, in truth, is the 'Word made flesh' in us."

Against these arbitrary and contradictory opinions the Church teaches, first, that, God's existence being already known by reason, the appointed channel of faith is not by interior revelation to individual souls, but by the word of other men, who speak to us in

[1] *Anleitung zum gottseligen Leben.*

God's name. Secondly, that their authority so to speak, or the fact and infallibility of this external revelation, must be apprehended, not by another interior revelation, nor exclusively by the operation of grace, but by reasoning and reflection on the evidence it presents. This is defined in the following terms by the Vatican Council. "In order," it says, "that the obedience we exercise in faith may be conformable to reason, God willed to combine with the interior aids of the Holy Spirit external proofs of revelation, namely, divine facts and pre-eminently miracles and prophecy. For these, being clear manifestations of the infinite power and knowledge of God, are the most certain signs (certissima signa) of a divine revelation, and are adapted to the intelligence of all."[1]

The history of God's dealings with men confirms the Church's teaching on this point. It shows from the beginning, that while the revelation was of course delivered immediately to its first preachers, whether prophets or Apostles, it was only indirectly and through their lips made known to mankind at large, and that the preachers themselves appealed to signs and wonders as proof of their divine authority. Thus Moses attested his mission by miracles; our Lord Himself appealed to His "mighty works" as a proof that He came from God, and the Apostles follow His example. St. Peter, in his first sermon at Pentecost, shows, both from the fulfilment of prophecy then accomplished in the visible outpouring of the Spirit, and again from the miraculous

[1] *Const. I.*, cap. 3.

resurrection of Christ, that the Jews were bound to believe in Him as the Eternal Son of God, and in the Apostles as His appointed heralds. The heathen had not the prophets, but they had the evidence of God in their own conscience and in external nature; so St. Paul at Lystra, after proclaiming by miracles his divine authority to speak, exhorts his hearers "to be converted to the true and living God, who made the heaven and earth, and left not Himself without testimony."[1]

The early Christian Apologists followed the same line. "We desire to prove," says St. Justin, "that not without reason do we honour Jesus Christ as the Son of God."[2] Reflection on the evidence offered is, with the Fathers, the appointed means of learning Christian truth. Origen repels indignantly the reproach of Celsus that the Christians believed blindly what they were taught, without any previous inquiry. "Such a charge," he says, "is more fitly brought against the Pagans, who attach themselves to philosophers from a mere fancy, in which reason has no part."[3] "Examine," says Tertullian, "if Christianity be true, and if belief in it be found to produce reformation of life, then it is your duty to renounce false (deities)."[4] Clement of Alexandria shows how knowledge prepares for faith. "We do not say," he writes, "that there is no truth without philosophy, or that it is the cause of Christian knowledge, or, again, that it contains the matter of revelation itself; but we hold that it is a preparation

---

[1] Acts xiv. 14-16.
[2] *Apolog.*, i. 13.
[3] *Cont. Cels.*, l. i. n. 11.
[4] *Apolog.*, c. 21.

for faith, and co-operates in its attainment."[1] Faith itself being, as he elsewhere says, a gift of the Holy Spirit.

St. Augustine, in various of his writings, describes clearly the function of reason in the assent to the motives of credibility. "First," he says, "we must find the true teaching authority, and must choose between those who adore a multitude of deities and the worshippers of the One God. Secondly, among the various worshippers of the One God that system is to be preferred whose divinity has been attested by visible miracles, and history shows that this was the case in the foundation of Christianity. But now miracles are no longer needed, for the world-wide spread of the Catholic Church is a visible sign of its divinity."[2]

It is noteworthy that the Apologists appeal rather to the fulfilment of prophecies than to the evidence of miracles in proof of the truth of Christianity. And their reason is twofold. First, essential as was the difference in their nature and results between the miracles of Christ and the Apostles, and the lying wonders of magic, as Origen points out, yet the former are constantly ascribed to occult or diabolic agency, an hypothesis impossible in the case of prophecies, where authenticity and antiquity were alike beyond dispute. No oracle or pythoness had ever attempted to foretell clearly and distinctly the distant future, as the Seers of the Old Covenant had with regard to

[1] *Poed.*, i. 6. Ed. Potter, p. 115.   [2] *De ver relig.*, c. 25.

Christ, and Christ Himself as regards His Church. Secondly, the evidence for miracles, though historically complete and thoroughly credible, was not so immediately apparent to the unlearned as were the vitality and diffusion of the Church, which was present and patent to all.[1] "The heathen," writes St. Athanasius, "reproach us with the shame of the Cross. They fail to see the might which is manifested among all the nations of the earth. For, through the Crucified One, the whole world is filled with the light of the knowledge of God."[2]

The most fitting proofs of our faith, or the motives of credibility, as they are otherwise called, are then found in the external evidence of its divine authority; viz., miracles, prophecies, and the supernatural life of the Church. Interior supernatural communications may justify the individual to whom they are addressed, in believing doctrines thus subjectively attested, but a teacher, claiming to speak to others in the name of God, must be prepared to show proof in support of his claims. In default of such proof, neither the moral obligation of believing, nor indeed any logical defence of religion, could ever be established.

Yet the Apologists in every age have made use of the interior evidence for Christianity, and this in two ways. First, *negatively*, they show that Christian dogmas, though they transcend, do not contradict the

---

[1] St. Augustine, *Cont. Faust.*, l. xii. c. 45 ; l. xiii. c. 7. St. Justin, *Apolog.*, i. 30.
[2] *Cont. gent. Orat.*, n. 1.

truths of reason. For, since God is the Author both of reason and revelation, systems which, like Mahomedanism, are based on immorality and imposture are necessarily false. And *positively*, the divine origin of Christianity is attested if its doctrines, incomprehensible though they be, are shown to supplement and complete the truths of reason. Dogmatic theology, indeed, is mainly occupied with these two points. The sacred science shows, first, that the objections, historical or philosophical, urged against revealed truth are apparent, not real; and secondly, by deducing conclusions of reason from premisses which are revealed, it defines and develops in human terms the doctrines themselves, while it illustrates the natural truths connected therewith in the fuller light of faith.

The gain to mankind of the knowledge thus acquired is too often ignored. Without theology, God is indeed known by the light of reason, but how imperfect, partial, and false is the conception of the Deity thus obtained. Contrast the isolated, repellent, sphinx-like, necessitated Being, called God in merely human religions, with the idea of Infinite intelligence, love, and Beatitude, personal and self-existent, manifested to the humblest child under the dogma of the Ever-blessed Trinity. Or compare the vague, shadowy notions of a future state with the definite, practical, and momentous teaching conveyed in the Christian doctrine of heaven and hell. Or again, how tender, reassuring, consoling, and yet consonant with the claims of divine justice and mercy, is the dogma of forgiveness of sin through the atonement of Christ, in comparison with any other scheme of retributive justice.

Similarly, the certainty even of our primary experimental knowledge is secured by revealed doctrine. While the external world, with all that it means to us, is either, according to the idealist, a phantom show, or with the materialists, soulless clay, the distinction of substance and accident, as defined in the doctrine of the Holy Eucharist, teaches the believer to affirm both the reality of what he sees, and the actual objective existence of the essence which is hidden to sense.

The examination of the doctrines of Christianity is, then, of much importance, yet the evidence presented thereby is not a strictly demonstrative proof of their credibility. The harmonies which are found to exist between reason and revelation presuppose the faith. They serve, therefore, as has been said, to confirm belief, not to determine the act of assent; rather, they develop the "intellectus ex fide," which is the reward of believing. The most that can be proved from the holiness or sublimity of Christian doctrines, or from their congruity with our needs, is the probability, not the certainty, of their revealed origin. But the fact of revelation must be proved with certainty to warrant the consequent assent of faith, and for the purpose of that assent, merely probable grounds are wholly worthless. And this certainty is obtained, when it is seen, first, that the historic proof is complete, that is to say, that the facts on which the Christian religion is based really occurred; and secondly, that these facts were in themselves clearly supernatural.

On the evidence of these two facts, then—the reality and the supernatural character of the origin of Christianity—the external proof of revelation rests. And to this proof the sceptic objects, that it necessarily moves in a vicious circle, being an attempt to prove one supernatural event by another, both of which are by their nature wholly beyond the cognisance of reason. Yet the objection is wholly groundless. For while some supernatural events are not susceptible of any direct natural test—for instance, transubstantiation, which produces no external sensible effect—there are others which are only effected by a cognisable change in the natural order, as for instance the multiplication of the loaves, or the raising of the dead; and to the latter class the miracles belong which are adduced as proofs for the fact of revelation.

What proof is there, then, that these miracles really took place? The evidence for such occurrences demands, indeed, a severer criticism than that required for ordinary events; but if the evidence offered in their behalf is thoroughly credible, and gains strength with time, and if, further, there is no natural explanation possible of the events in question, or of their results, then no ground remains for disbelieving the reality of their occurrence save the purely arbitrary and irrational assumption of their impossibility. Now, the Gospel narrative offers proofs of its credibility beyond those of any secular history. Wholly unlike the myths of Paganism, the product of a race in its far-off infancy, the Gospels record contemporary events, and were circulated among the most cultured people within and beyond Judæa, who could easily have exposed any false statement these documents contained. Yet no single note of protest was raised against their authenticity or truth. Nay, their main facts are supported by contemporary historians, Pagan as well as Christian, and their universal acceptance is justly regarded as an irrefragable proof of their veracity. Further, as the Church has in all ages maintained the authenticity of the Gospels, if the Church can, *on other and independent grounds*, prove its divine origin, then its official, circumstantial account of that origin must also be true.

But, it may be asked, if the grounds for faith be so certain, how can the assent of faith be still freely formed? Here, then, we must distinguish between evidence and certitude, and the relation of both to the will.

Evidence, then, is defined as that quality, by means of which an object is necessarily manifested to the mind or sense if their attention be directed thereto. By the object is to be understood, not the thing fully comprehended, but only so far as it forms the subject-matter of the cognition in question. Thus the outline of a body may be evident while its colour and properties are still hidden. Further, it is plain that anything becomes evident, not because of its intrinsic reality or truth, but by its being perfectly apprehended by the cognitive faculty. Now, it is proper to evidence, as thus defined, to produce not only knowledge, but such knowledge as compels our assent; that is, it manifests the object so clearly that we see not merely its nature fully, but that it could not be otherwise, that it necessarily is what it is.

It is otherwise with the certitude which enters into the assent of faith. This certitude is not necessary but free; that is, it is determined, not by the object alone, but by the immediate impulse of the will, and it has to be shown that we can be reasonably certain of the motives of credibility, that is, so as to exclude any fear of error, yet without such evidence as compels the assent.

We arrive, then, at this certitude, free and not compulsory, when the truth is so plainly manifested that any further doubt, though not impossible, would be unreasonable. Circumscribed as we are by space and time, complete evidence is offered us of but few things, and but for the power of arriving at reasonable certitude in default of such evidence, the truths absolutely necessary for human life would be beyond our reach. But this is not so. The faculty of judgment, which we possess as reasonable beings, enables us to distinguish what is certain from what is merely probable, and then to decide without fear of error. All inductive reasoning proceeds in this way. From the uniform recurrence of certain concrete facts, under given circumstances, we infer the existence of an universal and necessary cause, and hence conclude that as often as these circumstances recur the facts will follow. But as the cause itself is never manifested, how is the conclusion authorised? Not so much from the number of facts observed, but rather from their cumulative force, from the consideration, namely, that the experience already formed is confirmed by every fresh observation. By a similar process the laws of human conduct, and the greater portion of our human knowledge, rest on certitude not evidence, on a free not a compulsory assent.

It is objected to the trustworthiness of this free or moral certitude, that since it implies imperfect knowledge, as the bounds of knowledge are extended, its value is proportionably diminished, and that much that was regarded as certain in the distant past has proved untenable at a later date. To this it is answered, that though certain judgments, based upon insufficient or *primâ facie* examination, have obtained credence for a time, as, for instance, the circular movement of the heavens, and have subsequently proved erroneous, there is no trace of any conclusion, deliberately formed and universally accepted by mankind as true, which has afterwards been found untenable.

With this distinction, then, in mind between evidence and certitude, theologians teach that the proofs offered for the fact of revelation or the motives of credibility are certain but not evident—that is, they are not so cogent as those which attest the discovery of America and compel assent, but they are of equal weight with the testimony presented for the death of Julius Cæsar, of which event doubt, though unreasonable, may still exist. The obscurity, therefore, essential to the assent of faith, arises not only from the incomprehensibility of the doctrines revealed, but from the fact of revelation itself being not irresistibly, though certainly manifested. Were the latter apprehended with absolute clearness, then the consequent assent of faith would be natural and necessitated, and devoid alike of freedom or merit, as is the case with that of the devils. The demons with their superior intelligence cannot doubt that God has spoken, but because their assent is forced, their homage is servile and involuntary; they only "believe and tremble."

We can now see both how doubt in matters of faith is always possible, and secondly, how the obligation of believing always binds. That amount of proof is given to the inquirer, sufficient to convince him of the fact of revelation, if he approach the subject with the humility proper to a creature of limited knowledge, and to a sinner seeking at all cost forgiveness of sin. But this proof is insufficient, if he demands more evidence than is suitable for one in his dependent and subordinate position, and in the state of probation in which he is placed. Search, then, as he will, he will never find the truth. He has made for himself "eyes that see not, and ears that have no hearing." It was so in our Lord's time. To the Jews was granted the certain proof of His Divinity; yet they reviled His miracles as Beelzebub's, and persecuted the witnesses to their truth. It is so with the Church now. She may fulfil every prophecy, verify every note of a divine teacher, but it is always possible to question the genuineness of her sacred documents, the divinity of her origin, or the unity of her faith, and then to find no conclusive proof of her being more than a human system.

And yet the obligation of believing remains ever in force. And why? Because of the imperative character of a divine message. The credibility of human testimony renders it possible, but not obligatory, to believe in the facts thus attested. There is no moral duty to decide on the rights of York and Lancaster, or on the authorship of Shakespeare's plays. But in the case of a divine witness it is far otherwise. Our dependence on God is so absolute, constant, and necessary, that if we have credible motives for believing He has spoken, our assent then becomes a primary and imperative obligation. Analogously, as children are bound to honour and love those whom they have credible reason for believing to be their parents, because the law to honour father and mother is already in possession, so is it as regards the duty of believing in God's Word, but with this difference. A child may be mistaken as regards his supposed parents, but nevertheless he still fulfils his duty in honouring those who, at least nominally, occupy their place; just as every man is bound to succour his neighbour who is in apparently extreme distress. In both these cases the obligations of filial piety or fraternal charity are to be discharged, even at the risk of possible deception, for were it necessary to wait for complete proof, these primary duties would constantly remain unfulfilled. But the assent to this fact of revelation or the motives of credibility must be determined by no merely probable proof, however strong, but by the *most certain* signs, divine facts—especially miracles and prophecy—and these are offered to all. And when once these proofs are realised in their full force, and it becomes certainly credible that God has spoken, then there arises an evident obligation of accepting both the fact and the matter of the revelation thus attested on the authority of God.

It has been stated above that the assent of faith must be more certain than that determined by any natural evidence, even, for instance, the evidence which the primal verities of reason bear with them. Yet experience seems to prove the contrary, for we are often exposed, as regards the doctrines of faith, to involuntary doubts, which could never arise in the case of self-evident truths. To this it is answered that, in knowledge which we possess with certainty, two things must be distinguished. First, the clearness with which the object is manifested to us; secondly, the firmness with which we assent. To a merely natural, intuitive certainty, *e.g.*, the excess of a whole to its part, our assent cannot be firmer than the intuition which is its cause; but a moral certainty, such as precedes the assent of faith, being immediately dependent on the will, can always be increased in proportion to the motive which determines it. And thus it follows that, though self-evident truths are most clearly, nay, indubitably seen, and revealed doctrines are but obscurely manifested to us, our assent to the latter is more firm, because of the reverence and homage due to God, their Author. The precept of faith is in this respect like that of charity. We are bound to love God more than parents or friends "appretiativé"—that is, we must be prepared to sacrifice our attachment to every creature for love of Him. But we are not obliged to feel that love more "intensivé," such an obligation being incapable of fulfilment. Parents and friends, like self-evident truth, are immediately cognisable to us, and their presence necessarily determines our emotions or judgment; but God, His goodness and His truth, are alike known only through the veil of creatures, and do not necessarily affect sensibly heart or mind. It may be added, that as the well-ordered natural love for any creature, so far from being a hindrance, prepares, with the help of grace, for the love of God, so does any natural truth we possess dispose us, if supernaturally assisted, to accept the revealed Word.

Lastly, it may seem difficult to understand how, if the fact of revelation be so clearly cognisable by reason, the assent of faith, which is so immediately connected therewith, is yet wholly supernatural. The question, it must be premised, is wholly external to the essential points at issue between Catholics and non-Catholics of any shade. All theologians are agreed, first, as to the reasonableness of the assent of faith; secondly, that the motives of credibility are so clear as to render unbelief inexcusable; and thirdly, that faith justifies, as the beginning of our supernatural life. But as to the precise mode in which reason and grace co-operate in forming the assent of faith, theologians differ. We shall then, as heretofore, take F. Kleutgen as our guide.

Grace, then, he says, is in a true sense creative, in that it confers new and wholly supernatural powers on the soul; yet it is non-creative, in that the subject of its operation, the soul and its faculties, already exists. Secondly, supernatural operations are said to begin immediately or absolutely, even though the subject they perfect has been previously prepared by grace. Charity or justification, even more than faith, proceeds wholly from grace, for it *necessarily* regenerates the whole inner man. Yet it is preceded by successive supernatural preparations, as the Council of Trent defines, viz., faith itself, salutary fear, hope, with the beginning of love; finally penance, with the purpose of receiving baptism and beginning a new life—all which preparatory acts in no way lessen the supernaturalness of the justification which follows. So also faith has its antecedent supernatural preparation. First, the prevenient grace, "pius credulitatis affectus," inspiring the mind and will to attend to the motives of credibility, and to the fact that God has spoken. Secondly, the habitual grace of faith, strengthening the soul to assent to what He says, and to adhere with loving submission to that assent "super omnia." Again, as in the soul, thus endowed with the grace of habitual faith, reason is still operative in an apparently natural manner, though its considerations, judgments, and conclusions have attained a wholly supernatural character by the gift possessed, so may our previous natural knowledge of the motives of credibility be supernaturalised, without our being conscious of the fact. The assent of faith, then, formed by reflection on the motives of credibility, would be supernatural, first, as regards the subject-matter—God and His operations, in so far as they transcend reason; secondly, because it proceeds from a desire for the supernatural object and end; lastly, because reason and will are raised to a wholly supernatural efficacy, corresponding to this end—the assent to God speaking, and the voluntary adhesion thereto.

The foregoing remarks show that faith stands midway between the dim natural knowledge obtained of God from creatures, and the clear vision possessed by the blessed, who gaze on Him face to face. For by faith we know Him indeed as He is, but without sight, through His external word, wherein the created and the uncreate are, after a manner, united. The facts to which the Church appeals, in proof of her claims, are indeed finite and created, but of such kind that in them, though through a veil, God's supernatural government may be seen, and Christianity clearly recognised as a divine work. This kind of revelation is adapted to the condition of our earthly existence, and to the mode of apprehension proper to faith. As in this life we apprehend the intelligible idea under the sensible object and the spiritual soul under the material body, so must we recognise the divine teacher in the visible Church, with its human ministers and sensible Sacraments. But as our soul alone, without the light of reason, could never find aught intelligible under things of sense, so neither could we apprehend a divine revelation from its external facts without the aid of grace. That man may attain to revealed truth, grace must present it in its reality to his intelligence, must inspire the desire of its possession, and strengthen his reason to assent and his will to adhere thereto. Finally, as sense knowledge is a necessary preliminary condition, though not a cause of intellectual cognition, so does natural knowledge precede faith, though the assent and the habit alike are from a wholly independent and supernatural source.

REVEALED RELIGION

CHAPTER I

POSSIBILITY OF REVELATION

IN a previous volume it has been shown that the existence of God, as the one personal Creator and Rewarder, is made known to all men by the use of reason, and that the value and purpose of life depend on our apprehension of this truth. Our best and highest thoughts, our ideals of truth, purity, and holiness, our desire for happiness infinite and eternal, are idle dreams, unless they are realised in the living God.

Yet the knowledge, great though it is, gained of God from His works, is limited, inferential, and unsatisfying. We desire to know more of Him, of what is His inner Life and Being, of His thoughts and purposes as regards ourselves. No finite intelligence can answer these questions. The thoughts of our fellow-men are inscrutable, still more is the mind of the Eternal. But as by the uttered word mind can speak to mind and heart to heart, why cannot God communicate with His creature in some infinitely higher, and yet more simple way? He whispers to us through the medium of external nature, in the history of the past, through the dictates of our conscience; is it inconceivable that He will complete the work He has begun, and hold personal intercourse with creatures made in His own image? God is our Father, and we are His children. Of His Paternal love He has enriched the visible world with every variety of form and colour to gratify our senses; will He refuse our soul its highest desire, or grant it only what is strictly necessary, the knowledge of natural truths, and the finite discoveries of our own unaided efforts? Thus reason teaches us to expect a revelation; and revelation introduces us to a new realm of knowledge, above all that science or philosophy can teach, the kingdom of supernatural truth.

And if we consider the intimate mode of God's presence and action in our souls, as theology teaches it, the possibility of revelation becomes still more apparent. One human intelligence can only act on another *mediately* and externally by intellectual argument or moral persuasion; but God acts upon mind and will *immediately* and from within. In the order of nature God, as the first efficient cause, has given every creature not only its being, but its powers and action; He preserves these powers, enables them to go forth into act, and gives to them their particular mode of action, just as the instrument cuts in a straight or circular line through the direction it receives from the workman.[1] Even human experience

---

[1] *St. Thom. de Potent.*, q. 3, a. 7; S. I., q. 105, a. 5.

confirms at times this metaphysical truth. "Whence ideas come to me," said Mozart, "or how, I cannot say; I see them all in my mind at a glance; I hear the whole at once."[1] "At the early age of four years he began to write music which was found wholly in accordance with the rules of composition, though he had received no instruction in them. And in after life the whole of a symphony would develop itself in his mind, the separate instrumental parts taking their separate shapes, so to speak, without any intentional elaboration. Thus the whole of the overture to Don Giovanni was written out, though doubtless previously composed, in the night before its performance, which took place without any rehearsal."[2] As then in the mind of a great composer, the power of God can quicken the knowledge of the properties, relations, and dependencies of sounds, of new and possible combinations, and thus enable him to exercise, as it were, a creative art; so through the gift of faith, God can illuminate the soul and empower it to see all things in a higher unity by the light of revealed truth. Thus He opened the minds of the Apostles "to understand the Scriptures."[3] And this He could do at any time, and in any way, for "the Spirit breatheth where He will, and thou hearest His voice."[4]

Belief in a revelation, or in a divine message of some kind, is found in the traditions of all nations;

---

[1] Mozart's *Autobiography*, by Schlosser, 3rd ed., p. 122.
[2] Carpenter, *Human Physiology*, p. 607, ed. 1855.
[3] Luke xxiv. 4, 5.   [4] John iii. 8.

and the earnestness and depth of their religious life is proportioned to the intensity of this belief. A religion founded solely upon an intellectual contemplation of nature and of God, that is, a purely natural or philosophical religion, is indeed possible, and within the range of man's natural powers, as has been shown. But history knows no example of the kind. The manifold religious systems of the past vary in their higher or lower metaphysical aspect, their moral worth, their creed and worship; yet all alike believe in a primal revelation, however debased or obscure its tradition may have become—all acknowledge and revere God as the Founder of their religion.

The objections raised in our day against the possibility of a revelation have been long since anticipated and refuted. Strauss[1] says that "a revelation is an isolated act of God in time, which contradicts His immutability." But if God be the first cause and the primal mover of all that is, animate and inanimate, material and spiritual, and while remaining unchanged in Himself, causes these manifold changes in His created effects, according to His words, "My Father worketh until now, and I work,"[2] then, His immutability having been unaffected by the addition of each successive grade of being, there is no reason why He should suffer change or alteration by endowing intellectual creatures with the supernatural truths of revelation. Nor does a subsequent revelation betray either an original imperfection in the constitution of man, or

[1] *Glaubenslehre*, i. p. 274 ff.　　[2] John v. 17.

"a want of foresight on the part" of the Creator, for it is in the highest degree congruous with the wisdom, power, and love of God, to confer upon those creatures who are made in His own spiritual likeness, in such time and manner as He will, those higher gifts of grace which will enable them to share in His own essential glory, and participate in life eternal.

Again, " the immediate action of the Supreme Being on the human mind" in no way "implies the absolute passivity of the latter." For the one system which has ever taught and defended the independence (relative) of the human mind, and the responsibility attached to every human act, is that which maintains most strenuously the absolute dependence of every creature upon the power and will of God. For the divine premovement acts on each class of being according to its nature, and preserves, nay alone causes, their independence and individuality.[1]

Again, the fact that the doctrines of revelation are already fixed does not "exclude human speculation and investigation thereon." The objects on which our senses act are fixed, but this does not forbid their examination by the scientist; nay, it is precisely their predetermined certainty which gives a secure basis to his investigation. The first principles of every science are fixed, and because they are so they form the laws which regulate and test every true advance in each branch of knowledge. For the same reason, then, because the subject-matter of revelation is divinely

[1] *De Potent.*, q. 3, a. 7.

certain, theology can securely occupy itself with illustrating, confirming, developing, and applying the truths it contains.

Lastly, Strauss objects, "How can we recognise any revelation as truly from God, and not a delusion?" "Before a man believes," says St. Thomas, "he must see that the matter proposed for faith is worthy of credence on account of the evidence of signs or such like things."[1] A revelation is therefore always attested by accompanying infallible marks; miracles in the physical, prophecy in the moral order, are the external test and guarantee of its truth. The Catholic Church has always insisted that the proof of what is interior or spiritual must depend first on the proof of what is exterior or visible. Thus in philosophy it condemns a purely subjective system of thought as tending to the construction of an *à priori* ideal world, and maintains that the certainty of our intellectual judgments presupposes the certainty of our sense experience. So, in religion, it condemns the idea of an exclusively interior spiritual creed, and maintains the necessity of a visible Church as the sole certain guarantee and witness of spiritual truth and good. "An authoritative teacher," says St. Augustine, "demands faith, and thus prepares the believer for the scientific examination of the doctrine taught, and for some understanding of its meaning. But 'to believe on authority' a previous exercise of the intellect is necessary, in order to decide on the credibility of the teacher. Thus we gain know-

[1] S. II. II., q. 1, a. 4, ad. 2.

ledge in two ways, by authority and by reason. In the order of time authority comes first, but in the order of things reason. At first sight authority appears the best adapted for the masses, and reason for the learned; but, in fact, authority alone opens the way to all who wish to arrive at the highest science. After we have accepted truths on authority, we find them, later on, to be solidly based on reason."[1]

Thus it is that revelation quickens, develops, and perfects two desires implanted in us by nature, the desire of knowledge and the desire of faith. We see this effect obtained in the instruction which the Church imparts. The Catechism contains the elements of the most sublime philosophy, and yet the humblest child who accepts its teaching is enabled to solve problems that perplexed the mightiest intellects unaided by grace. Divorced from knowledge, faith degenerates into superstition and fanaticism, as was the case with the Pagan nations of old, or in savage tribes, or in Mahomedanism in later times. On the other hand, mere secular knowledge without faith produces scepticism. Such has been only too often the effect of non-Catholic civilisation on the Jew or the Hindoo, who have learnt to abandon the creed of their birth without being taught where to find definite religious truth. So, again, the spirit of inquiry, the thirst for knowledge, apart from faith, among civilised people, begets a kind of mental atrophy which is always craving, yet

[1] *De Ord.*, ii. 9: *De vera relig.*, xxiv. Cf. *De Moribus Eccles. II. contra. Academ. I. III.*

never satisfied, "ever learning, and never attaining to the knowledge of the truth."¹ Men of active mental temperament are especially subject to this evil. Too soon they find themselves at the term of human thought and speculation, and keen is their disappointment when they realise how little they know compared to what they do not.

> "I feel it, I have heap'd upon my brain
> The gathered treasures of man's thought in vain;
> And when at length from studious toil I rest,
> No power, new-born, springs up within my breast;
> A hair's breadth is not added to my height,
> I am no nearer to the Infinite." ²

And now let us consider the reasonableness of believing in mysteries. Every truth which transcends reason is a mystery to man. Such truths meet us alike in the moral and physical world. Those ethical principles which all men regard nowadays as the highest, the value of self-sacrifice, the love of enemies, belong to an ideal standard, which our fallen reason could never have reached.

Again, in the physical order, how many mysteries confront us? How much do we comprehend of the nature of light, heat, and force, of which we speak so often? Light, the medium in and through which visible things are alone manifested to us, is itself so mysterious in its principle and nature as to be absolutely unknown. Again, "Force and matter," says

---

[1] 2 Tim. iii. 7.
[2] Goethe. Swanwick's *Faust*, Part I. p. 58.

Helmholz, "are mere abstractions."[1] "Natural science is limited by the impossibility, on the one hand, of understanding matter and force, and on the other, of comprehending spiritual processes."[2] "I know," said Newton, "the laws of attraction, but if you ask what attraction is, I really cannot tell." In fact, man only comprehends what he has made himself. Thus he understands the mechanism of a clock, because it is his own work; but though he can dissect the dead body, and resolve it into its constituent parts, yet life escapes his scrutiny.

> "The parts he holds, but ah !—the soul
> Is fled that made those parts a whole."

Thus are we surrounded by mystery. "When a man hath done," said the wise man, "then shall he begin, and when he leaveth off, he shall be at a loss;"[3] and from these mysteries there is no escape. The Atheist who denies the existence of God, because he cannot comprehend the nature of an omnipresent, eternal Being, is confronted with the insoluble enigma of a world existing without a cause. The Pantheist who will not admit the fact of creation, because he cannot comprehend the production of being from nothing, must accept instead the absurdity and contradiction that the infinite and the finite, the temporal and the eternal, are all one and the same.

[1] *Ueber die Erhaltung der Kraft*, p. 63.
[2] Du Bois Raymond, *Ueber die Grenzen des Naturalismus*, 1873, p. 29.
[3] Ecclus. xviii. 6.

But how, it is said, can we believe what we do not comprehend? To comprehend is a figure borrowed from sensible objects, signifying to take round, compass, embrace. Thus we comprehend a body, if we know perfectly all its dimensions and constituent parts. In its metaphysical sense, it means to know a thing as fully as it can be known. Thus too, intelligence signifies "intus legere," to read within, and implies an inner, intimate knowledge, which, in its perfection, is for man impossible. Perfect comprehension and perfect intelligence belong, therefore, to God alone, in whose word we believe, when we accept the mysteries which He reveals. But these mysteries, though beyond, are not contrary to reason. " Although," says St. Thomas, "the doctrines of the faith surpass the truths of human understanding, there can be no opposition between them. Both proceed from God in their respective orders of grace and nature. And the doctrines of faith become as indubitable, through the evidence of the divine authority revealing them, as the primary truths of reason do through their self-evident testimony."[1]

"Thus," says also St. Augustine, "if reason seek to establish any doctrine which is contrary to the authority of Holy Scripture, such doctrine can only be true in appearance; and, on the other hand, if any doctrine be put forward as of faith, which is opposed to the certain and self-evident truths of reason, such doctrine cannot be in reality a proposition of faith, but is an individual and false opinion."[2] This necessary and

[1] *Cont. Gent.*, i. 7.   [2] *Ep.* xliii. *ad Marcell.*

enduring agreement of faith and reason, because of their common origin from God, the one sole fount of immutable eternal truth, whether natural or revealed, has been defined by the Church in our own day;[1] while the contrary proposition of Pomponatius, that a doctrine could be true in philosophy and false in theology, was condemned by the Sorbonne in the sixteenth century.

But the obligation of believing in mystery is based on a higher reason than the limited nature of our understanding. Man is ordered to a supernatural end to which he cannot attain unless it begins to pre-exist in him in some way now. That end is eternal life in God, and life in God consists in the full knowledge of God.[2] Our reason teaches us with certainty, from His effects, that God is; what He is we know only inadequately and in a human way. The full knowledge of His inner being, His nature, and person, and attributes, and all those unfathomable mysteries which are absolutely and necessarily beyond the range of human reason, can only be learnt from God Himself; and the *beginning* of this knowledge can come to us only in a supernatural way, and by the infused light of faith.[3] Hence belief in mystery is the form and principle of all true religious life. A religion, in fact, without a revelation is not worthy of the name.

A revelation, again, which only declares what we

---

[1] *Conc. Vat. de fide Cath.*, cap. iv.
[2] John xvii. 3.
[3] *De ver.*, q. 14, a. 2. Cf. a. 10, *Conc. Vat. de fide Cath.*, cap. iv.

already know, or might discover for ourselves, has neither meaning nor purpose. "The rationalist," says Schelling, "while retaining the word revelation, restricts its matter to certain pure and lofty truths which could have been naturally known, but which were taught by the founder of Christianity as a teacher endowed by Providence in order that mankind might become earlier possessed of them. But since, according to them, these truths were revealed in so obscure a manner that it has taken ages to dispel their obscurity, the benefit of revelation is thereby denied. But the truth is that either revelation has manifested what would otherwise have remained unknown, or no revelation has taken place."[1]

Belief in mystery is then strictly accordant with reason, and great are the blessings it brings. The intellect, in accepting what it cannot understand, on the sole authority of the Word of God, does homage to the divine veracity, and acknowledges God's supremacy in the realms of thought as the one absolute, essential, and eternal truth. For an assent of faith is determined, as has been said, not by evidence of the truth of the doctrines proposed, but solely by evidence of the truth of the teaching authority. That evidence, as regards the authority, is clear, but as regards the doctrines revealed is essentially and always obscure. Hence, it is always possible to refuse to believe, and an act of faith must always be preceded by an act of obedience, the voluntary and reasonable,

[1] *Philosophie der Offenbarung Gesamm. W. W.*, Part II., vol. iv. p. 5.

ILLUMINATION OF FAITH 39

but not compulsory, submission of the will to God speaking. It is this submission of the will which renders faith meritorious, while the contrary act, the wilful refusal to believe in spite of sufficient evidence, makes unbelief a sin. Its guilt consists in the deliberate denial of the truth of God's Word, and the deliberate preference of human reason as the more trustworthy authority.[1]

Faith, however, while demanding the complete and abiding submission of man's reason, is no enslaving thraldom. On the contrary, no act is so cognate to the nature of the intellectual faculty as that by which the mind is brought into immediate and direct relation with the source of all truth. Illuminated by divine wisdom, the mind distinguishes realities from appearances, detects error under its manifold disguises, and obtains a marvellous comprehensive grasp of truth. For the mysteries of faith, though incomprehensible, are not insoluble enigmas to be learnt by rote and mechanically repeated. In their grandeur, beauty, and truth, their mutual relations, and their complete agreement and unity, they are the highest, most pregnant, and instructive objects that the mind can contemplate. " We ought to consider by the light of reason," says St. Augustine,[2] " what we firmly hold by faith, and that not merely because of the illumination of the understanding which follows therefrom, but also for

---

[1] St. Aug., Tract lxxxix. in Joan.
[2] " Quæ fidei firmitate jam tenes, etiam rationis luce conspicias " (*Ep* cxx. ad *Consent.*).

the sake of the wonder and admiration, the affections and higher desires which such study enkindles. Why then do we seek, it may be asked, to know more of such a subject as the Holy Trinity if we really comprehend that it is incomprehensible? We can only reply that it is impossible to cease, since as long as we search into these matters, incomprehensible though they be, we grow better and better from the mere fact of seeking so great a good. For when found it is sought anew, and in the seeking is ever found. For when sought it is found to be ever more sweet, and when found it is the more eagerly sought for. And in this sense those words of Ecclesiasticus may be understood: 'Those who eat me shall yet hunger, and those who drink me shall yet thirst.'" [1]

Nor is it only the invaluable knowledge of divine things which this higher wisdom imparts; the God of nature and of grace is one and the same, and the two orders correspond. The sacred mysteries present therefore analogies to the natural order, and find expression in visible symbols and earthly counterparts, while innumerable truths, principles, and forces of nature are only fully understood when seen in the light of revelation. On the vantage ground of faith man stands above the mists of falsehood, and sees in their various deformity the aberrations of the human intellect, from the rudest degradation of fetish worship to the latest refinements of Agnosticism. The same lofty eminence of supernatural truth discovers to him those principles

De Trin. xv. 2.

which solve the problem of his existence, the heights and depths of his own complex and mysterious life. Here, too, the history of the world, to fallen man so meaningless and chaotic, is seen in its sequence, order, and purpose, and all human actions, even the most criminal, are found to co-operate for the great end of creation, the glory of God, and the salvation of souls. As the streams which fertilise the valleys flow from some hidden source in the heights above, and as all the prodigal wealth of foliage, flowers, and fruit which nature displays is produced by forces working unseen in the womb of the mother earth, so all the best treasures of human life, all that supports the strain and weariness of its daily conflict, all its true wisdom, good, and happiness, have their source in the obscure but illuminating mysteries of the faith.

Hence, faith in mystery is both reasonable and beneficial, and it is by belief in mystery and dogma that the greatest triumphs of civilisation have been achieved. And of what kind was the world over which faith triumphed? It is the fashion now to extol Pagan morality and virtue, yet in that heathen world cruelty was the rule and revenge a duty. It was a world in which the blood of thousands glutted the appetites of brutal multitudes, lust held its orgies under the midday sun, the temples of the gods were sinks of vices, and creatures of infamy the sacred ministers. In that same world despots reigned without law, and slaves obeyed without conscience; pride reached its apogee and a licentious tyrant was raised on the altars and adored as God; and this world, then decaying and corrupt, had only before it a deathbed of despair. True, it had a civilisation, but a civilisation without God; and though art had attained its highest perfection, and could portray the noblest idea of outward man, tranquil and beautiful in its exact symmetry and just proportion, yet the lips of the idol were mute; it expressed no sign of faith, or hope, or charity, but of a spirit doomed and enslaved, which quailed before the dark fate which even the gods could not escape.[1] And into this world of death the Spirit of God breathed a new life, and the dry bones lived again by faith. Its triumphs may be briefly summarised—the creation of the individual man, the abolition of idolatry and of slavery, the ennoblement of woman, the maintenance of civil and political rights, of individual freedom, the distinction between the spiritual and temporal powers, the idea of an education universal and gratuitous, the duty of submission to authority, of tending the sick and needy, of self-sacrifice and charity. Whence came either the thought of such principles as these, or the power to carry them into effect? From dogma only; from the mysterious and incomprehensible dogma of the Incarnation of the Son of God, of the Word made flesh. "After we had believed in the Word," says St. Justin, who was led by philosophy to Christ in the beginning of the second century, "our life became entirely transfigured. Once we took pleasure in unseemliness, now we only desire chastity. Once we

[1] Staudenmaier, *Encyclopädie der Theologie*, p. 197.

practised magical arts, now we serve the Most High, the uncreated God. We used to covet gain and riches above all things, now we have all things in common, and share what we possess with the needy; we hated each other and were always at strife, now we regard even strangers as our kin, and pray for our enemies."[1]

This, then, is the victory which overcometh the world, our faith. By faith the believer possesses the germ and the foretaste of a future life, which develops from grace to grace till it finds its consummation in the Vision of God. "He who believes has life eternal."[2]

[1] *Apoloy.*, l. 51. [2] 1 John v. 13.

CHAPTER II

THE NECESSITY OF REVELATION

THE history of mankind is the history of its estrangement from God, and the consequent loss of the true idea of religion. Offspring though he was of race divine, man soon forgot his supernatural destiny, bowed down before idols, and worshipped the work of his own hands. Thus a dark night of superstition and idolatry covered the earth, and its spread, density, and duration have been accounted for by many conflicting theories, alike opposed to truth and to the essential dignity of human nature. Some, as the Materialists, find in the idolatry of earlier times, and in the degradation of existing savage tribes, a proof that reason is but a development of the brutes' sentient faculties, and regard the idea of God as one phase of human thought speculating on the cause and law of natural phenomena. Others again, from the same fact of man's ignorance, have denied that he could ever have arrived by his own reason at the idea of God, and have maintained that every notion of religion and morality was only obtained by a revelation from God. The advocates of this theory are called Traditionalists, since it teaches that all primal verities of which we are possessed depend for their certainty not on reason, but on tradition of some kind; these truths being handed down either— according to Ventura and others—by the "sensus communis" of mankind, or—according to de Bonald, by the gift of speech. The office of philosophy, therefore, was not to demonstrate the certainty of these primal truths, but, assuming them as proved, to deduce what conclusions followed therefrom; just as theology presupposes as certain its premisses, which are *de fide*, and only develops the truths implicitly contained therein. This dogmatism in philosophy destroyed, as must be apparent, every rational motive for belief in natural religion or morality. For if the existence of God and other essential truths depended only on tradition and were incapable of proof, how was the sceptic to be answered who denied the existence of that tradition? and further, if our primal verities depended on tradition and not on reason, we should have had no reasonable motive for being certain of anything. The theory was, moreover, self-destructive; for as regards the school of Ventura, what test was there for each individual man that the "sensus communis" was true, if he were in himself fallible, and incapable of judging either of the truths proposed, or of the veracity of the authority which taught it. Further, the "sensus communis" which was to be regarded as infallible, was only in fact the collective wisdom of so many fallible individuals. On the other hand, had this primal revelation been conveyed by language, as de Bonald held, then speech would have been but an accidental endowment of man, and not his essential characteristic as a reasonable creature. Again, since according to this theory speech was prior to thought, how would man ever have understood the meaning of the terms revealed? Again, in the very nature of things, the mental word—verbum mentis—precedes its outward utterance—verbum oris—just as in physical generation conception is prior to birth. Thus speech everywhere appears as the expression of thought, and the rudest languages, as well as the most highly organised, exhibit a marvellous order and logical development. "The dialects of the Indian tribes," says Duponceau, "appear to be the work of philosophers rather than of savages."[1] In his primal innocence, indeed, man was divinely assisted to name all the things before him, but in his normal state he forms his speech gradually, but naturally and for himself, as new objects are presented to him, or new ideas are conceived. It is thus that Dante describes speech as the joint effect of necessity and freedom:

"That he speaks,
Is nature's prompting; whether thus, or thus,
She leaves to you, as ye do most affect it."[2]
Parad., c. xxvi. v. 129.

We have dwelt thus much on the Traditionalist theory, since it denies what we have been endeavouring to establish,[3] that every man has by his own reason, apart

[1] Tholuck, *Verm Schr.*, ii. p. 260. [2] *Parad.*, cxx. vi. v. 129.
[3] See *Natural Religion*.

from revelation or tradition, the certainty of God's existence and of the first principles of intellectual and moral truth. The need which man has of a revelation, as regards the knowledge of God in the order of nature, and the fulfilment of the moral law, is relative not absolute, moral not physical. Wounded though he be in his fallen nature, man's will still has sufficient strength really and physically to do what is good, and his intellect sufficient light to persuade and induce it so to act. Neither faculty has lost any of its intrinsic power by the fall, for the entity of both remains entire and intact. The weakness of will and the mental ignorance to which man is subject proceed from an external impediment, the attraction which objects of sense possess for his lower appetites, and which is so urgent, close, and disproportionate that reason scarcely if ever asserts its rightful sway. Hence arises an impotence to see and do what is right, which is moral but not physical, a necessity relative, not absolute, for divine revelation to establish as certain what was, *per se*, within the power of reason to learn for itself. "The hand of man," says Suarez, in illustration of this truth, " is physically capable of drawing a circle, yet would never succeed in doing so with mathematical accuracy without the help of a compass." [1]

Let us then examine whether unaided reason has as a fact ever attained that knowledge of moral and religious truth which is needed to give purpose and stability to human life. If it has never done so, the

[1] *Disp. Theol.*, tom. i. tract ii. lib. ii. cap. 15.

failure must be due to the fact that such a task is beyond the natural capacity of man as he is, for a power or faculty that can never be exercised in act, is at least morally impotent, or for practical purposes does not exist.

We find our question answered by one who speaks with authority as regards the state of religious knowledge in the Roman world. Cicero, writing " De natura Deorum," says, " The question concerning the nature of the gods is so difficult and obscure, and the opinions of the most eminent writers are so diverse, that we cannot justly yield any assent to them."[1] Notwithstanding the great natural gifts of those who made religion their study, and the earnestness of their efforts, the result was perplexity and doubt. Pre-Christian creeds present, indeed, traces of the formal universal tradition concerning the creation of the world, the existence of God, a judgment to come, and a future state; but these truths are almost wholly obscured by the addition of false and superstitious fables. Sublime and instructive doctrines are transformed into degrading myths, and the highest spiritual ideas are represented by gods and goddesses whose imaginary lives are stained by monstrous vice. This appears in a marked manner in the public worship of Pagan times. Its essential characteristic was sacrifices offered, with priesthood and altar, and accompanied by an elaborate ritual. Now sacrifice expresses the primal truth of the sovereignty of God,

[1] *De nat. Deorum*, i. 13, iii. 40.

and ritual, the fear, reverence, and care due to all that appertains to divine worship. Yet the sacrifices of heathen worship were but too often of human flesh and blood, its concomitant ceremonial merely an incentive to lust, its deities were idols of man's own make. Not only among the Tyrians and Phœnicians, the Canaanites and the Carthaginians, but in Athens and Rome, as in Africa and South America in our own day, human blood was poured forth on the altar of idols. "The Romans," boasts Pliny, " cannot be sufficiently esteemed for having everywhere prohibited human sacrifices and cannibalism, which were considered acts of piety."[1] Yet "even in our own day," writes Tertullian, A.D. 200, "human blood was offered upon the altar of Jupiter Latialis in the midst of the city;"[2] and again he declares that in the time of the Proconsul Tiberius children were sacrificed openly to Saturn in Africa, and that the soldiers who were charged with the deed could bear witness to the fact.[3] No less degrading than this inhuman cruelty were the frightful obscenities which accompanied the worship of the idols, and which the heathen mythology encouraged. Against the foul rites of Moloch and Baal, and the Pagan gods, with which the Jews were too apt to be contaminated, prophet after prophet, Jeremias, Ezekiel, Nahum, cried aloud. These degrading rites, with their attendant priests and priestesses, represented the only form of popular creed. The priests had no higher office than that of ministering

[1] *Hist. nat.*, XXX. 12.   [2] *Scorpiac.*, c. 7.   *Apoloy.*, ix.

to the idol worship; they had no disciplinary, judicial, or teaching authority or office. Religious dogma, in its true sense, was unknown. The myths had been first cast into form and then handed down, not by priests, but by the poets. And the immorality of their legends is condemned in the strongest terms by the sages of old. "Homer," says Heraclitus, "deserves to be excluded from the popular assembly."[1] Xenophon declares that "Hesiod and Homer imputed to the gods all human vices, theft, adultery, treachery."[2] "Homer," says Cicero, "transferred human things to the deities; would that he had brought divine things to us."[3] Religions founded on such a teaching could not possibly elevate or improve the masses, who were its principal adherents. The people, as a whole, had no more instruction in morals than in dogma. "The Pagan divinities," says St. Augustine, "wholly neglected the lives and morals of the cities and nations who worshipped them, and by no dreaded prohibition hindered their becoming utterly corrupt, nor preserved them from those terrible and detestable evils which visit not harvests and vintages, not house and possessions, not the body which is subject to the soul, but the soul itself, the spirit that rules the whole man. If such prohibition exists, produce it, prove it! Purity and probity, they say, were inculcated upon the initiated, and secret incitements to virtue were whispered in their ear; but this is an idle boast. Let

---

[1] *Diogen.*, lib. xi. 1.   [2] *Sext. Empir.*, ix. 193.
[3] *Tusc.*, i. 16; cf. *De nat. Deor.*, iii. 21.

them show or name to us the places where, instead of the obscene songs and licentious plays, the celebration of those most filthy and shameless Fugalia (well called Fugalia, since they banish modesty and right feeling), the people were commanded in the name of the gods to restrain avarice, bridle impurity, and conquer ambition. Let them name to us the places where such instructions were wont to be communicated from the gods, and where the people who worshipped them were accustomed to resort to hear them, as we can point to our churches, built for this purpose in every land where the Christian religion is received."[1]

In the vague hope of finding some higher or purer creed, many more earnest souls travelled in various lands, had themselves initiated into the divine mysteries, and made trial, as far as possible, of the whole circle of existing creeds. Thus Plato traversed Greece and Egypt to discover the best religion. But the gods of each land in turn proved but the embodiment of some imaginary local legend, dramatised by the people to serve as the pabulum of their passions and the instruments of self-love. Each system bore its own narrow and national stamp, and each contradicted the other; and so scanty and conflicting, so extravagant and improbable, were the results of these travellers' search, that they seemed, as Cicero says, "the wild phantasms of a visionary rather than the teaching of a sage."[2] Hence, wearied and disappointed, the master spirits of those Pagan times, convinced of the hope-

[1] *De Civ. Dei*, ii. 6.   [2] *De nat. Deorum*, i. 16.

lessness of a conflict against the prevailing ignorance and corruption, could only exclaim with Tacitus that life was but "one huge comedy and the world a dream."[1]

Yet idols still held their sway, nor did the philosophers ever dream of disputing their supremacy. Religion was a state necessity for the contentment of the masses, and the forms of creed or the number or kind of deities were matter of national taste or custom, which had grown up with time, and could not be safely disturbed. Since a religion was needed, and philosophy had no religion of its own to offer, no statesman, however sceptical he might be, would interfere with or disregard the popular rites. "Personal conviction," says Cicero, "must be distinguished from civil observance."[2] In other words, think what you like, but worship as the law prescribes. Even in Plato's ideal state the traditional Hellenistic religion is to be alone permitted, and its forms of worship were to remain unaltered. In doubtful points the Delphic oracle might be consulted.[3] Xenophon, again, makes it a point in his defence, "that he had never sacrificed to other gods than Jupiter and Juno, and their kindred divinities: by these alone he had sworn, and in these only he believed."[4] Nor was it only from a motive of political expediency that even the sceptical Pagans thus paid homage to the gods. The history of those times shows, what the records of later ages uniformly confirm, that infidelity constantly begets childish and

---

[1] *Annal.*, iii. 18.   [2] *De Legg*, ii. 10, 12.
[3] *De Repub.*, iv. p. 427.   [4] *Memor.* 24.

degrading credulity. Even though God did not exist, or His existence was at best uncertain, still men could not divest themselves of the thought that powerful superhuman agencies were operating in human affairs, for the most part with malignant purpose, and that it was at least prudent to propitiate their favour. Thus says Cicero, " Wherever you turn, you are met by superstitions; it may be a soothsayer, an augury, or a sacrifice; you have seen a bird, or have met a Chaldean or a magician; or it has lightened or thundered, or something out of the common happens, so that you never find rest."[1] And this superstition infected all classes. Tiberius kept a soothsayer in attendance; Piso employed magical arts against Germanicus; at the prediction of a magician Galba made his attempt on the empire. Vespasian was supposed to work miracles and cure the blind; while for destructive purposes the art of poisoning, as Tacitus relates,[2] came to the aid of magic to secure its results.

And when all means failed to win the favour of the gods, or obtain the desired end, the same superstition manifested itself in acts of puerile and petulant vindictiveness. Thus, after a naval defeat, Augustus punished Neptune by ordering the removal of his statue. At the death of Germanicus, the images of the gods were broken, as an act of retribution, in many cities of Italy. On these and similar facts even Renan remarks: " How nations more advanced in civilisation than ourselves could bow down before

[1] *De Divinat.*, ii. c. ult.   [2] *Annal.*, ii. 69.

sensuous and intemperate deities, and find in absurd and scandalous stories the substance of their religion, is to us incomprehensible. Is it not strange to find a people gifted with genius like the Greeks, or capable of carrying out a scheme of policy by which they became rulers of the world, like the Romans, yet in the sphere of religion almost on a level with the rudest Fetish worshippers? How could nations who are our models in municipal and political life, in art, philosophy, and poetry, have remained satisfied with a religion whose absurdities would be apparent even to a child's understanding?"[1] And in all time the same phenomena recur. The triumph of the Reformation and the consequent loss of faith coincided with the rise and spread of witchcraft. It was in Protestant countries that the black art held its sway. The enlightened sceptics of the French Revolution, who denied the existence of God, yet believed firmly in evil spirits of all kinds; and the books of the National Library most read, says Pourtalis,[2] at that time, were those which treated of sorcery and magic. Countries like Japan and China in our own days exhibit at once a merely natural civilisation in some respects very advanced, coupled with slavish superstitions in matters of belief. As free thought in Europe advances we see in our own time table-turning, spirit-rapping, clairvoyance, and hypnotism in turn obtain popularity.

[1] *Etudes d'histoire religieuse*, pp. 7, 8.
[2] *De l'usage et de l'abus de l'esprit philosophique*, vol. ii. pp. 127, 171.

But it may be asked if the religious systems founded on fable and myth produced such baneful results, why did not the philosophers of antiquity find the truth, or at least the most important verities, and proclaim them to the people? And the answer is furnished for us again by Cicero, to whom the study of philosophy was a labour of love, and whose writings give us an impartial summary of the teaching of the different schools. The result, then, of his exhaustive researches was briefly, that there was nothing too absurd for a philosopher's creed;[1] a remarkable confirmation of the Apostle's words, that "professing to be wise, they had become fools."[2] Concerning the soul, he says, "God alone knows which of these opinions is true; nay, it is hard to determine which is the most probable."[3] Again, "About the nature of the gods this is what I had to say to you. I do not mean to deny their existence, but would have you understand what great obscurities and difficulties the treatment of the question presents."[4] And the reason which he assigns for this uncertainty in the supreme problems of life shows how thoroughly he understood the obstacles encountered by fallen man in the pursuit of truth. "Nature," he says, "has granted us but faint sparks of knowledge, and since these are soon extinguished by our immoral habits and vices,[5] the light

---

[1] *De Divin.*, ii. 58.   [2] 1 Cor. i. 20.
[3] *Qu. Tusc.*, i. 11.   [4] *De nat. Deor.*, iii. 39.
[5] "Those men that detain the truth of God in injustice" (Rom. i. 18).

of nature in its clearness and brightness is nowhere to be found. True, the germs of virtue are implanted in our minds which might have guided us to eternal life. But from our birth we live in a singular atmosphere, infected with false opinions, so that we imbibe error almost with our mother's milk, and our teachers lead us so utterly astray that truth must yield to outward show, and even the voice of nature is stifled by deeply-rooted delusions."[1]

And if we turn to those teachers whose systems approached most nearly to the truth, and which were appealed to by the Fathers in their polemics with the heathen in support of certain natural virtues, how imperfect, erroneous, nay, immoral, they appear viewed by the light of the Christian revelation. Even Plato, the most Christian of the old philosophers, was doubtful about the fact of creation, and taught an essential opposition between idea and reality, and that body and soul were separate substances, and were only related as a ship to the pilot, or the horse to his rider. His doctrine of innate ideas has given birth in subsequent ages to many false systems, notably in later times to the idealism of Descartes. And when we turn to the doctrines of charity and purity, the sanctity of the marriage-tie, his moral doctrine is seen to be abominably corrupt. He recommends the exposure, *i.e.*, destruction, of weakly children, community of wives, and tolerates "paiderastia;" while by upholding slavery he condemns the whole of the third

[1] *Qu. Tusc.*, iii. 1, 12.

order, or the great majority of the population, to unconditional servitude.[1]

And if the ignorance and uncertainty of the philosophers on the most important questions, no less than their irreconcilable contradictions, disqualified them as the teachers of mankind, such a task was made more impossible by the scandalous character of their actual lives. "How many philosophers are there," says Cicero, "whose morals or way of living are such as reason requires? Some are so frivolous and fond of display that it would have been better for them to have learnt nothing. Some are covetous, others are ambitious, others the slaves of lust, so that their actions are always contradicting their words, which seems to me the most despicable of all things."[2]

Lastly, no ancient philosopher, however learned or moral, could ever have been the teacher of men, for his learning was not for the multitude. Knowledge, Plato taught,[3] was for the few, for those who were truly freedmen by birth, and it would be profaned by being made common. When Alexander the Great reproached Aristotle for having revealed his mystic doctrines to the people, the latter replied that "he had indeed published these doctrines, but had never revealed them." His published exposition was intentionally so obscure as to be unintelligible.[4] Truth was only to be obtained as the reward of learning, of

---

[1] Cf. Platon's *Werke*, Bd. iv., *Einheit zu Phäd*, von Steinhart.
[2] *Qu. Tusc.*, ii. 4.   [3] *De Repub.*, vi.   [4] Plut., *Alex.* 7.

mental superiority; and the poor, the uneducated, or those who had no time or aptitude for study, were excluded from its possession. The fundamental tenet of Gnosticism, that the mysteries were only for the initiated, has been continually reaffirmed by the learned of this world.

So in our own day, Schelling[1] took for his motto the "Odi profanum vulgus et arceo" of Horace. The Hegelian school divided mankind into two classes, the learned and the simple believers; truth was for the former, myths for the latter. Renan, who also had a "dédain transcendant" for the multitude, says that "it is given but to a few to soar above in the higher spheres of knowledge, and that those who do so are content to fly by their own wings, and care little how the rest understand their God."[2] Nay, he puts forward as a plea for the sufferance of religion that it meets the wants of those who are incapable of being elevated by science, and supplies them with some sort of an ideal. And of what value would be a religion thus formulated for the popular use? Based on sentiment, devoid of any objective truth, it would be, as its advocates teach, but a form of religious instinct which, though true in itself, is variable and contradictory in expression. And yet these transient delusions are all that the teachers of science can find for the support of the great mass of mankind in its greatest need.

---

[1] *Vorlesungen über die Methode des academischen Studium*, p. 111.
[2] *Etudes sur l'histoire religieuse.* Preface.

As far, then, as the history of human thought extends, there is no trace of unaided reason ever having provided any education for man in the true sense of the word. In physical science immense progress has been made in modern times; truths have been established, laws and principles demonstrated, discoveries multiplied, which tend to minister to the material comfort and welfare and ease of man; but philosophy deals with the whence and the wherefore, the origin and the end of things. Its office is to call wisdom down from Heaven, to tell man what to do, and how to do it; and here, where truth is most necessary and is needed by all, modern teachers fail as completely as any in bygone times. "It is the nemesis of independent thought," says Hegel, "that every system produces something more absurd than its predecessors."[1] To the teachers of to-day the words of St. Peter fitly apply: "The feet of those who shall bury thee are at the door." From despair of ever attaining to truth arises the belief that there is nothing but what meets the senses, and from Materialism the human mind recoils in disgust to the vague and shadowy contradictions of Pantheism, to be again thrown back to the god of matter.

Nor do these teachers themselves deny that they have failed. But we are to have confidence; we must wait, the sun of science is but rising; in the philosophy of the future every enigma will be unravelled, and all things made clear. Altruistic

[1] *Geschichte der Philos. Einleitung.*

humanity, education, the franchise, each and all, are to regenerate mankind and renew the face of the earth, only time is required. Is this, if true, consoling to us now? Life is short; will death wait for the promised triumph of science? Every second of time a soul passes into eternity; what of the countless multitudes who have already made the passage; what of ourselves if death finds us still waiting, still in doubt, still undecided as to truth? Such a death has no hope, and opens to a future equally hopeless, " for man's salvation, as God has ordained, depends entirely on his knowledge of truth."[1]

Is there, then, any system which teaches truth, teaches it with authority, and to all? Yes, one voice, and one only, teaches now and always " with authority and not as the scribes." Christ " learnt no letters," but He taught " what He had seen in the Father,"[2] for " He and the Father were One."[3] He was Himself the Truth, and His teaching was therefore infallible and immutable. " Heaven and earth might pass away, but His word never." And this teaching taught the whole circle of truth needed for man's salvation, the beginning and end of all things, the purpose of existence, the nature of body and soul, the meaning of suffering, temptation, and trial, the secret of life and death, and beyond this, the nature of God, His hidden Being, and the mysteries of Heaven. And what Christ taught the Church teaches still, and her teaching is for all. While the study of philosophy

[1] S.I., q. 1.   [2] John viii. 38.   [3] John x. 38.

was restricted to the intellectual or learned few, the heavenly wisdom was opened to Greek and barbarian, slave and freedman, the rustic and the philosopher alike.

The prophet's words were then fulfilled, that "all thy children shall be taught of God, and great shall be their peace."[1] And even the heathen scoffer bore involuntary testimony to its accomplishment. Celsus reproaches Christianity for addressing itself to fishermen, to the poor, to the most miserable, and for inculcating the love of slaves, those beings of a lower order, of whom the gods had no account.[2] And this same fact the Christian apologist appeals to as a proof of the divine power of his religion; not only could the poorest learn the dogmas of faith, and moral principles transcending the highest philosopher's standard, but they made those doctrines part of their being, and incorporated them in their lives. "Among us," says Athenagoras,[3] "you will find ignorant people, and men and women of the labouring class, who, though unable to put into words the saving power of their religion, yet exhibit its effect in their hearts, not by eloquent phrases, but by good works. When struck, they strike not again; they suffer wrong, and seek no legal redress; they give ever to those who ask them, and love their neighbours as themselves." "It seemed," says another, "that all Christians were in truth philosophers, or that all philosophers had be-

---

[1] Isa. liv. 13; John vi. 45.   [2] *De morte Peregin.*, ii. p. 597.
[3] *Legat. pro. Chr.*, n. 11.

come Christians."[1] And this was indeed the case. What truth the Pagan had, the Christian possessed still more abundantly, unmixed with error, and purified and made perfect. The Christian revelation has been the one source from which every subsequent teacher has drawn his best ideal and highest principles, however indignantly he may have repudiated belief in its dogmas. "I know not," says Rousseau to Montaigne, "why the beautiful moral of your writings should be attributed to the progress of philosophy, for this morality is taken from the Gospel, was Christian before it was philosophic."[2] "We grant," again writes Kant to Jacobi, "that if the Gospel had not first taught the moral law in its purity, human reason would never have grasped it in its completeness."[3] When, in the year 1797, La Reveillière Lepeaux, one of the five Directors of France, laid before the Institute the scheme of his new religion, "Theophilanthropy," Talleyrand remarked; "I have only one thing to remind you of; in order to found his religion, Jesus Christ was crucified, died, and rose again; you must see how you can do the same."

What has been said is sufficient to show the need of revelation. But in addition to a fixed authoritative teaching in dogma and morals, Christianity supplied man, as no other system could, with a ritual and worship in every way worthy of his faith. Pagan sages had, we have seen, tolerated, nay, supported,

---

[1] *Minutius Felix Octav.*, c. 20.   [2] *IIIme Lettre de la Montaigne.*
[3] Jacobi, *Werke*, p. 322.

the heathen ritual and sacrifice, in order to satisfy the religious feelings of the masses, but no attempt was made to purify these rites of their cruelty and sensuality; for the philosophers knew no higher truth which could be manifested in outward form. Their theories of God, the soul, and eternity were too difficult and abstract for any audience but those of the school and the portico; they could never form ideals for the artist, the sculptor, or the poet; nay, the sages themselves feared, lest, by becoming more definite in their teaching, they might profane what they spoke of. "Thou seest," says Socrates to Plato, " that thou canst not worship God with any certainty, since thou must fear lest He may reject thee for having uttered a blasphemy. Therefore it seems best to me to wait patiently till one comes who will teach us what our bearing should be towards God and man."[1]

Now the great central truth which Pagan philosophy was incapable of teaching, and which the heathen sacrificial worship expressed only in perverted form by occult and abominable rites, was the offended majesty of God, or sin and the need of atonement. The consciousness of guilt, individual and personal, and of a guilt which must be punished, was universal. No heathen ever denied that a nemesis hung over the heads of mortals, no sophistry ever banished this belief from men's minds. The attribute of God which was most clearly manifested to man in this fallen world, apart from revelation, was not His mercy but

[1] *Alcibiades*, ii.

His vindictive justice. This is what was seen in sorrow, trial, pain, death, above all in the secret sting of conscience and the worm of remorse; and these witnesses were patent and living and in every life, while the signs of the divine compassion were transient and occasional. How then was satisfaction to be made; what are the conditions for forgiveness? According to modern ideas, sin and its consequences are very easily disposed of, and by man himself. By amendment of life and sinning no more, says the Rationalist, we do the best penance for the past. Spinoza would have us find peace by conscious union with the Infinite; Rousseau, by returning to pure unsullied nature, and so regaining an idyllic perfection.

All these might do, were sin a dream which fades with returning consciousness, a passing indiscretion, or again only a natural and necessary defect. But the sting of conscience, after the sinful act has ceased, proves the malice of sin and the voluntariness of its nature. The brutes cannot sin, because they are governed by necessity, are moved only by natural impulse, and have no choice. But man is intelligent and free, he can choose this or that; and it is precisely in the free, individual preference of his own will to the will of God, that the malice of his sin consists. How, then, is he to escape the punishment which necessarily follows? Nothing in nature can save him, for nature herself, with every creature, is stained through sin, and groans under the servitude of corruption. And again, it is to God that satisfaction is due, and God is not a weak ruler, who modifies His laws when they are infringed, or threatens, but never strikes; or an indulgent parent who pardons repeatedly and without reason, and finds excuses where none exist.

The heathen knew this; they knew that the divine justice was inexorable, and that satisfaction must be made for the outrage done. They sought, therefore, some victim, the best they could offer. Human life was the most precious of all, therefore they offered human sacrifice; but every human creature was stained by personal sin, and as the brute creation fell only indirectly under the curse, the heathen offered also vicarious atonement by the blood of bulls and heifers, in the hopes that it might be more acceptable because more innocent. Thus the priest prays in Ovid:

"Accept this heart for heart; these limbs for limbs we give;
Thus giving life for life, a better life to live."
—*Fast* vi. 161.

Or, again, in the later times of heathenism, a strange rite was invented, combining in a manner both human and animal sacrifice, but without destruction of human life. In the Taurobolia the carcass of the slain ox was placed on a perforated slab, under which lay the penitent. There he remained till he was covered with the blood of the victim, when he arose purified and sanctified to be venerated by the people.

But the blood of goats and calves was powerless to pay the debt of sin. "The penal effect of sin on every

E

individual soul, after the act itself had ceased," says St. Thomas, " is threefold. By the deformity of sin the soul loses the beauty of sanctifying grace and incurs a stain. Secondly, its natural good is corrupted, for the whole nature of a sinner is disordered by the fact that his will is not subject to God. Thirdly, the soul is under the debt of punishment, for the man who sins mortally merits eternal damnation."[1] And this threefold evil was blotted out by the passion and death of the God-man, Christ Jesus. By His essential holiness the image of God was renewed again in the soul with the dignity and beauty of which sin had deprived it; by His obedience unto death the whole moral order was reinstituted; by His resurrection to eternal life Hell was closed and Heaven reopened to man. What, then, the Christian believed in, confessed and adored, was the one atoning sacrifice of Christ crucified, and this one mystery formed at once the central point of his faith and the visible manifestation of his salvation, and the idols and their hideous rites disappeared, to be replaced, from the rising of the sun to the going down of the same, by the clean unspotted sacrifice of the Immaculate Lamb.

But though Redemption was effected by the sacrifice of Christ, and Christianity made that Redemption intelligible to all, still man's nature was not changed; it still groaned under the burden of sin. Within every individual soul there still dwelt two opposing

[1] S. I. II., q. 109, a. 7.

forces of the old Adam and the new Christ, the one heavenly, tending to things spiritual, invisible, and eternal; the other clinging to things of sense, to the enjoyment of what, though transitory, is visible, present, and attractive. The materialising influence of the external world had not ceased because "the Word was made flesh," nor had temptation lost its power because human nature was regenerate in Christ. The prolonged, incessant conflict between the flesh and the spirit, which Plato described as being dragged by two steeds in opposite directions, and which convinced Xenophon that he had two souls, since his life was both good and evil, was experienced in all its force even by the great Apostle of the Heathen. How touching is his experience; broken resolves, abortive desires, hopes disappointed, failure in spite of the best endeavour—all are heard in that cry, "The good which I would I do not, the evil I would not that I do." And if St. Paul, infallible in truth and indefectible in grace, could speak thus with truth of his own inner life, what must be the experience of those —the great mass of mankind—who are neither apostles nor martyrs, and who, if not struggling with memories of past mortal sin, are labouring to make progress under a chronic load of tepidity. Terrible indeed is the warfare when evil presences approach so near—even but in imagination—that the inmost being is convulsed and every nerve quivers. Whatever its special form—hate, ambition, sensuality— what is offered and promised by the tempter at the moment is the immediate possession of every earthly bliss. Will rationalistic morality avail then? Of what power the frigid spectre of virtue against the fresh and fascinating reality of a living object? Of what efficacy philosophical maxim, dignity of self-respect, against a voice that pleads, against a touch that enthrals? When the tempter has wound his coil round the soul, so that it is passive and helpless in his grasp, who can overcome the poisonous reptile and cast it into the flame? The strong man is not overcome save by one stronger than he. Amid the storm of passion and the mist of false excuses and vain delusions, when the intellect is blinded and the will paralysed, one voice only can be heard—the accent of faith, the fear of God which speaks of Hell and its torments as the inevitable result of that perhaps momentary gratification, of Heaven as the reward of the soul that endures.

In those supreme moments in human life, when eternity hangs in the balance, the grace of Jesus Christ is man's only hope. The form of the God-man, the incarnate manifestation of Divine Truth and Love, in His majesty and humility alike ineffable, in His sternness and gentleness, in His infinite condescension, His purity, His self-sacrifice, and the divine grace flowing from His Passion and death—all these alone enable man to triumph over the assaults of evil. For in Him are found teaching and example, the Truth and the power to understand it, the Law and the means of fulfilling it, strength for sacrifice, and, even here, reward a hundredfold for the loss of all else, the goal to make for, and the only way thereto; for Jesus Christ is our Creator and Redeemer, our Beginning and End, and this revelation alone teaches, and faith alone secures.

CHAPTER III

MIRACLES AND PROPHECY

"GOD, who at sundry times and in divers manners spoke in times past to the fathers by the prophets, last of all, in these days hath spoken to us by His Son, whom He hath appointed heir of all things, by whom also He made the world."[1] From the beginning of the world, the Revealed word went forth to man with ever-increasing power: it developed new truths upon earth, inaugurated a new religion, and as the principle of a higher life among the nations, in the past as in the present, profoundly influences the history of mankind. Not, like a mythical religion, the poetic expression of a vague nature worship, nor, like a philosophical creed, evolved by human reason, Revelation, being a manifestation of the inner life of God, is a fact, effected solely by His divine will. On its external side it has indeed an historic development; the truth however announced, Revelation itself is in no sense determined by the course of events, but is, on the contrary, their determining cause. After centuries of preparation, the supreme and final end of Revelation was attained in Jesus

[1] Heb. i. 1.

Christ, the Incarnate Word, in whom the Wisdom of the Father dwelt visibly upon earth.

The purpose of Revelation being to elevate to a higher grade the order of nature, its forces correspond to those of the visible creation. As matter and spirit, by their natural properties and laws, point to the existence of a Creator, so miracles and prophecy attest, in the realm of matter and of mind, the fact of God revealing. In both nature and Revelation it is God who acts. In the order of nature the divine action is uniform, and so far God is hidden under the action of second causes; in Revelation, on the contrary, the divine action is extraordinary and exceptional, and thereby God is manifested as its immediate efficient cause.

Our purpose, then, in this chapter is to show that miracles and prophecy are possible, and capable of being proved. A miracle is defined by St. Thomas as "an effect of divine power, surpassing wholly the course of nature, or an effect of divine omnipotence beyond the power of any created cause."[1] It is distinguished therefore by three chief characteristics.

First, as an effect beyond the power of any creature; no event, however extraordinary, which is not supernatural, such as an earthquake or an eclipse, would be a miracle, though it might have that appearance to many persons.

Secondly, it must be operated in the natural order, though not according to its ordinary laws. Hence the effects of justification and the sacraments are not,

[1] Cont. Gent., l. iii. c. 101.

in the strict sense, miraculous, because they do not belong to the order of nature, but to that of grace.

Thirdly, according to many theologians, it must be an effect patent to the senses, its purpose being to cause admiration or wonder (whence the word *mirum* or miracle) as a sign of divine power. Hence the visible multiplication of the loaves was a miracle, and Transubstantiation, being invisible, is not.

Miracles are divided into three degrees; as they exceed the power of nature by reason of the fact itself (*ratione sui*); by reason of the subject in which the miraculous effect is produced (*ratione subjecti*); or by reason of the manner in which it is produced (*ratione modi*). To the first class belong the sun going back on the dial of Achaz, and the gift and condition of a glorified body, as our Lord's in the Transfiguration, for both effects are in themselves essentially beyond the whole power of nature. The raising of Lazarus, or the restoration to sight of the man born blind, belong to the second class, for though nature gives life and sight, yet not to the dead or the sightless. The descent of rain at the prayer of Elias, the restoration of Peter's wife's mother from the fever, belong to the third class, since they were miraculous by reason of the instantaneous manner in which they were produced.[1]

Such, then, are miracles, and their different kinds. Now, are they possible? What is the answer of mankind as a whole? History shows us that all nations

[1] *Cf.* S.I., q. 105, a. 8.

have some religion, and that prayer is its language and the expression of its life. But the very fact of prayer indicates the belief that nature and its laws are not unalterable in themselves, nor fetters binding the hand of God, but on the contrary, are the docile instruments of His omnipotence. Prayer assumes that He, as the Author of Nature, operates through her laws and forces, and also that He can modify, suspend, or change them at will; and it is in the divine action, operating independently of these ordinary laws, that a miracle, as has been said, consists.

Now this belief in the efficacy of prayer and in the power of God to hear and grant our petitions is strictly reasonable, and is in no way incompatible, as some have objected, with that eternal immutability which is one of His essential attributes. The plan of God's Providence is indeed certain and immutable. For while the creature, owing to its limited knowledge, can never be secure of attaining its purpose, God, by reason of His omnipotence, ordains infallibly all and each, the greatest and the least of the beings He has created, to their predestined end, the manifestation of His goodness in the universe as a whole. Defects in the material instrument, resistance or malice in the created agent, may indeed frustrate a particular good; but evil, whether physical or moral, is foreseen, permitted, and ordered to the universal good. Such is the divine plan in the Creator's mind. But it belongs equally to the completeness and dignity of God's Providence that, while one and unchanging in itself, it should be carried out by a number and variety of subordinate agents, unconscious and conscious, determined and free, who, according to their several natures and operations, accomplish His work. Now it is in the nature of rational creatures both intelligently to desire their perfection and to express that desire by prayer; and it is in accordance with the Providence of God, who has implanted that desire in His wisdom and goodness, to satisfy the same, in so far as it conduces to the creature's appointed end. Moreover, it is part of His Providence to use second causes, as has been said, in producing certain effects; and as He has made the harvest depend on the toil and care of the husbandman, and the stability of the house on the skill of the architect, so He has made certain other effects, the salvation of the soul and the diffusion of grace, depend on the prayers offered for these ends. But as neither the sowing of a field nor the building of a house changes the divine government of the world, but are preordained therein, so is it also with prayer. It is a necessary condition in the plan of God's Providence for the designed result, and has been so ordained, because thereby men are taught to recognise their dependence on God as their beginning and last end, and to appeal to Him with trust, while in granting what is fitly asked, the divine goodness and mercy to the creature are displayed.[1]

The fact of the supremacy and independence of the

[1] *C. Gent.*, iii. 95, 96.

Creator which prayer supposes, finds a parallel in nature by the dominion exercised by the superior over the lower order of Being. Every higher grade in the natural order stands towards the lower in a relation analogous to the miraculous—*i.e.*, it belongs to a new class of forces, and produces in the lower organisms effects beyond their power by which these latter are limited and transformed. The organic principle, vital force, overcomes and controls the action of the law of gravitation, suspends that of chemical forces, and directs them to their higher end, the support of life. As soon as the vital force quits the body these forces recommence their work of destruction. Every living being, " the stirring of the life-germ in the dead wood of matter,"[1] compared with purely chemical and natural forces, is a superior agent and power acting upon these lower organisms, but not produced by them. If we saw the stones by the wayside suddenly putting forth leaves and bearing blossoms and fruit, or the forest trees beginning to walk, we should at once admit that a miracle had taken place. Yet there must have been a time when the first plant appeared in a world of inorganic forms; when the first animal moved in a world of undeveloped organisms; when man appeared in the animal world, and his articulate speech first mingled with its inarticulate cries; when rational beings first began to hold mutual converse. These facts were then inexplicable by any hitherto known phenomena in any

[1] Jean Paul, *Levana*, i. p. 126.

former regions of nature. Surely these were miracles then, even if they have ceased, because of their constant repetition, to be miracles now. Man, with his life of intelligence and freedom, was the latest miracle of creation.[1]

A miracle is then a phenomenon in nature, but not the working of nature. To understand its fitness as the sign of a divine revelation, it must be remembered that all creatures have a twofold end, their own particular good, and secondly, the good of that universe of which they form part. And this "bonum commune" is attained by the graduated scale of excellence which the universe displays. From the lowest to the highest the inferior creatures are subordinate to the superior, and minister to their wants. The inanimate kingdom ministers to the animate, the animate to the sentient, and the sentient to the intellectual soul of man. And man himself attains his own perfection, and ennobles all the creatures under his sway, by finding in them ever new reasons for praising the wisdom, power, and love of the Creator. If, then, the visible creation is the means by which he is first instructed in the knowledge of God, it was consonant with divine Providence that extraordinary changes in that creation should bespeak a further manifestation of Him.[2]

There is then no impossibility nor unfitness in the fact of miracles. Now, let us consider the evidence

[1] *Cf.* Deutinger, *Renan und das Wunder*, Munich, 1864, p. 104.
[2] *C. Gent.*, iii. 99.

as to their occurrence. Consistently with their belief in the power of prayer, the ancients regarded miracles as an essential part of the divine government of the world, and the supreme manifestation of the Deity, and therefore looked for them as the pledge and seal of a message from Him.

Hence it was that when the Apostles went forth to proclaim Christ crucified throughout the world, and, before Jews and heathen, appealed to His miracles as evidence of His divine mission, the obvious objection, viz., the impossibility of miracles, which would have destroyed Christianity at once, was never raised. Celsus, Julian, and Porphery exhausted their ingenuity in opposing Christianity, and, above all, the divine wonders which attended its rise ; but, like the Jews with Christ, instead of denying their occurrence, they ascribed them to demoniacal or magical arts, or, with Julian,[1] to some occult natural or pathological science possessed by the Christians. So far was the possibility of miracles from being denied, that those of Pagan gods and heroes were appealed to as a counter evidence. Aristeas,[2] Simon Magus,[3] and especially the false Christ of later heathenism, Apollonius of Tyana,[4] were all alleged to have produced preternatural or magic effects. When the gods were silent their inaction was to be ascribed, not to fear, but to hatred.[5]

But it may be asked, granted that a belief in miracles

---

[1] *Cyrill. Alex. C. Jul.*, vi. p. 192. [2] Orig., *Adv. Cels.*, iii. c. 2.
[3] Iren., *Adv. Hær.*, ii. c. 31. [4] Lact., *Inst. div.*, v. c. 3.
[5] Ibid., iv. c. 27.

is universal, and miraculous effects are an accepted test of divine Revelation, is it not an argument against Christian miracles that every false religion boasts of similar wonders? To which we reply with Pascal,[1] that the existence of false miracles, far from disproving the existence of true ones, leads to an exactly opposite conclusion. A counterfeit implies a true original, and the false wonders of Paganism point of necessity to the occurrence somewhere of divine extraordinary intervention.

But if so, how are true miracles to be distinguished from "lying wonders"? First, then, as regards the fact of their occurrence; many of the Pagan miracles were said to have occurred in remote times, and were only based on poetic legends. The Christian miracles took place in the full light of history, in the presence of multitudes, and were attested by credible witnesses. Secondly, the Pagan miracles had no moral significance; they were powerless alike to build up or to destroy. They were exhibitions of the power of the operator, displayed solely for his own glorification. Thus with regard to the alleged miracles of Simon Magus, the author of the Clementine Homilies asks in the name of St. Peter, "What profit was there in his walking statues, his barking dogs of stone or brass, his transforming himself into a serpent or goat, his mountain ascents, or his flight through the air. All that proceeds," the writer continues, "from a good cause, has regard to man's salvation, such were our Lord's

[1] *Pensées*, part ii. art. 16.

works, the making the blind to see, the deaf to hear, the healing of the lame, the infirm and the sick, the expelling of devils. All these were signs to salvation, and to man's good in some way, and therefore beyond the power of any evil spirit." And often the purpose of these "lying wonders" was not merely frivolous, but immoral. "Any one could foretell," says Arnobius, "in what these machinations would result, the instilling of a deadly poison, the opening of locked doors, laming horses, making them weak or rendering them furious, depriving men of the power of speech, or exciting in either sex ungovernable lusts."[1]

True and false miracles are thus distinguished by the purpose for which they are worked, and the connection in which they are found. Divine wonders are effected solely to testify to the truth and to the establishment of God's kingdom on earth. This contrast is thus brought out by Origen. "What," he asks, "came of these (Pagan miracles)? In what did they issue? Where is the society which has been founded by their help? What is there in the world's history to show that they lay deep in the mind and counsel of God? The miracles of Moses issued in a Jewish polity; those of Jesus Christ in the Christian Church; whole nations were knit together through their help. What have your boasted Apollonius or Esculapius to show as the fruit of theirs; what traces have they left behind them?"[2]

---

[1] Arnob. *Adv. Gent.*, ii. 43.
[2] *Cont. Cels.*, i. 67. *Cf.* Trench, *Miracles*, Pref.

Thirdly, though evil men, such as Balaam and Caiaphas, may display supernatural power or knowledge, the character of the operator is, as a rule, a sure indication of the truth or falsehood of the wonders worked. When the agent displays love of the truth, zeal for God's honour, avowed antagonism to evil in any form, contempt of the world, and above all, obedience to authority, such signs show that the wonder is from God.

And now let us consider some modern objections to miracles. It has been urged by Spinoza and Strauss, that a miracle is a suspension of the natural law, and as, according to them, the natural law is the expression and product of the Divine Will, a miracle implies a contradiction in God.[1] First, then, nature undoubtedly works according to law, but this law is a fact, the proof of which rests solely on experience, and is not, like a mathematical proposition, an intrinsic, absolute, *a priori* necessity. All that we know of the uniformity of the natural law is that, as a rule, it is unchanging, not that it is unchangeable by any higher power. The truth of a mathematical proposition, on the contrary—the fact that three angles of a triangle equal two right angles—is unchangeable by Omnipotence itself. "Law," says even Moleschot, "is only the briefest or universal expression for the agreement of a multitude of phenomena. The law was never devised before the phenomena, but discovered by means of them." We admit then that

---

[1] Spinoza, *Tract Theol. pol.*, c. vi.; Strauss, *Glaubenslehre*, i. p. 229.

THE DIVINE IMMUTABILITY

miracles may be called a suspension of the laws of nature, but in the same sense as the lower forces are suspended by the action of superior forces in the ordinary operations of nature. As a magnet suspends the law of gravitation by retaining the iron in mid air, so God could make the axe-head swim at the bidding of Eliseus, without the magnet, by His own divine will. Man, it is true, must act within the laws of nature, as we know them; God can act outside them (præter ordinem naturæ). But in a miracle, He does not, strictly speaking, suspend a law of nature, but overcomes, in conformity with nature, a lower by a higher force. A miracle is therefore beyond nature, but not unnatural.

Still less is it true to say, with Spinoza and Strauss, that miracles contradict the divine scheme of the world, because miracles, as the extraordinary operations of God, were included from the beginning in the plan of His Providence. "The order of the universe," St. Thomas says, "can be considered in a twofold aspect. First, as regards those things which are subjected to that order and depend on second causes; and secondly, as regards the order itself, as dependent on its principle (the First Cause, God). Now as regards the things ordered, God could create other things wholly different, for His power is in no way restricted to this or that set of creatures; but as regards the order itself which is dependent on Him, God could not act in opposition thereto. For the order proceeds from the knowledge and will of God, ordaining all things to His goodness as their end, and God could not possibly do what He has not willed, nor will what He had previously disapproved, nor do aught which His providence had not from eternity decreed, for such a change would imply defect on the part of His knowledge and will. This distinction between Providence as existing in the divine mind, and its effects as manifested in creatures—the divine motive and the means by which it is carried out—is often overlooked, and hence have arisen divers errors. Some have taught that the immutability of the divine order in itself extends to effects dependent thereon, and that all creatures are therefore necessarily what they are. Others, on the contrary, have held that Providence itself changes with the changes in creatures; or that contingent things are wholly outside the order of divine Providence."[1]

And now let us consider the moral necessity of miracles. Revelation being, as has been said, a fuller manifestation of God than is found in the order of nature, it must necessarily be accompanied by supernatural acts attesting its divine truth. The teaching of our Blessed Lord, divine and holy though it was, would not have approved its divine origin, save to a few holy souls supernaturally enlightened to perceive it. Hence, miracles were needed to arrest the attention of the masses and of the indolent and frivolous, and to compel them to inquire into the claims of the doctrines which demanded the assent of all, and that

[1] *Cont. Gentes.*, iii. 98; cf. i. c. v. a. 6.

even at the cost of life. This authoritative claim on man's obedience, because of the proof which the Teacher Himself offered, was special to Christ's teaching. Philosophy sought to prove the truth of its doctrine by lengthy arguments ; " but Christian doctrine," says Origen, " relies upon its own evidence, a sure foundation far deeper than all the dialectics of the Greeks."[1] The apostle called this evidence, "the showing of the Spirit and power;"[2] of the Spirit, by prophecy ; of power, by miraculous works.

On the value of miracles as evidence, Rousseau says: "The faculties of men are so variously organised, that the same arguments affect them very differently. Accordingly, what is evident to one mind, seems barely possible to another. One is convinced by a certain class of truths, another by a different class. Therefore, when God gave to man a Revelation, which all men are bound to believe, He furnished it with the proofs best calculated to convince all men, whether great or small, learned or unlearned, wise or simple. The first proof is the nature of the doctrine; the second the character of the organ of the revelation ; the third that of miracles, as an expression of divine power, which is able to set aside the ordinary course of nature. This last is undoubtedly the most luminous, striking, and manifest proof of all ; one which needs least discussion or elaborate explanation ; and is especially calculated to attract the masses."[3]

[1] *Cont. Celsus.*, i. 2. [2] 1 Cor. ii. 4.
[3] *Lettre III. de la Montagne.*

The tendency then of certain writers, professedly Christian, to depreciate the significance of miracles, and, with Hegel [1] and Lessing, to affirm that "contingent facts of history can never be proofs for the necessary truths of reason," arises from a false conception of the nature of the Christian religion and Revelation. "St. Paul," observes Möhler, "whose apprehension of things is always spiritual, though so highly intellectual, insists upon the intimate connection between his faith and his conviction of the Resurrection of our Lord: 'If Christ,' he says, 'be not risen again, your faith is in vain.' And how could it be otherwise, since in Christianity, which is a positive divine religion, the idea and history, the inward and outward, are inseparable? But our idealists and spiritualists need no miracles to confirm their faith, because what they hold is their own opinion, not faith in Christ." [2] Pfleiderer confirms Möhler's words, unwittingly, from a Protestant point of view. "In our day," he says, "when the analogy of experience exercises so potent an influence over men, it is urged, that far from being an aid to faith, miracles are its greatest hindrance; and to many they are the rock which wrecks their faith. It is undeniable that, in the present day, most Christians believe, not because of miracles, but in spite of them; hence they have no longer any value as evidence." [3]

---

[1] *Werke*, vol. vi. p. 348. *Cf.* Lessing, *Werke*, vol. v. p. 80. Berlin, 1825.   [2] *Symbolik*, p. 318, 2nd edition.
[3] *Wesen der Religion*, p. 390, 1869.

But the question presents itself, how are we to recognise a miracle with certainty, how distinguish it from natural phenomena? Viewed in its external aspect, a miracle is a fact, perceptible to the senses, like every other fact of experience, and is therefore capable of proof, according to the ordinary rules of evidence. Its extraordinary character in no way invalidates the trustworthiness of the witnesses testifying to its occurrence, but only demands a stricter and more careful scrutiny, and the evidence, if found credible, should be accepted as true. If every event of an exceptional character is therefore to be rejected as incredible, there would be an end to history, and a subversion of the moral order of the world, upon which all human authority rests. Strauss,[1] however, quotes Hume,[2] to show that no evidence in support of a miracle can ever be credible.

Hume's argument is as follows: "The unbroken uniformity of the natural law is attested by a firm and unalterable experience, which nothing could upset but the evidence of infallible truth; and even then, the testimony being only of equal weight on either side, it would be the duty of a prudent man to suspend his judgment. But experience shows that the testimony of men is very often fallible, and hence the evidence in favour of a miracle can never be complete." Now these statements rest really on the assumption that the laws of nature are inviolable, and

---

[1] *Glaubenslehre*, i. p. 238.
[2] *An Inquiry concerning the Human Understanding*, sect. x.

this because of the second assumption that there is no evidence of any higher power which can control or change them. But what has been already said of the universal belief in the power of prayer shows that, according to human testimony, the presumption is in favour of the existence of a Sovereign, Omnipotent Creator, who can, and does, for a sufficient purpose, interrupt the ordinary course of nature. If, then, miracles be a natural pledge of the reality of a Revelation from Him ; if, further, there be a general expectation of, and an adequate purpose for such a Revelation, and if again, the events flowing from a Revelation so attested cannot be accounted for by any natural cause, and subserve a high and holy end, then, the argument in favour of the miracle having taken place is far stronger than that based on the *à priori* assumption of its impossibility. "The miraculous," says Zeller, " is an immediate consequence of Theism."

If, *per impossibile*, an effect satisfying all the conditions of a true miracle was operated in support of a false doctrine, the lie or deception would recoil upon the Creator Himself, and establish universal scepticism. It would be God Himself who had deceived us.

Nor is it the case that these two facts—that of the uniformity of natural laws, and that of the attested supernatural events—contradict and therefore nullify each other, for they essentially differ in kind. The natural event depends upon the natural law, whilst the supernatural is clearly due to a non-natural cause.

Hence the exception produced by a non-natural cause, far from contradicting, only serves to confirm the law of nature, viz., that purely natural causes produce uniform effects. " The affirmation," says Bonnet, " founded on the experience of past ages, that the dead do not rise again, is not in reality opposed to the contrary statement, if made by credible witnesses, that the dead have returned to life : for the one refers exclusively to the operation of natural, the other to that of supernatural causes."[1] Their difference, therefore, is based on different aspects of the same event. Nor, again, is the objection valid, that a complete knowledge of the laws of nature is necessary to determine with certainty that a particular event is wholly beyond one class of natural causes, and can only be produced by those of a higher species. Without a scientific knowledge of mechanics or of all the effects they may produce, we know that the life of a plant differs essentially from the movement of a watch ; and that no human power could ever produce the vital principle, which therefore points to its Creator as its cause. Though unable to point distinctly to the border-line between different species, we may be able to affirm unhesitatingly the essentials characteristic of both. The colours of the rainbow, dawn and morning, twilight and darkness, blend imperceptibly ; who can tell where the one begins and the other ends ? yet we can distinguish with certainty blue and green, day and night. Every man, again, however unskilled

[1] *Recherches philosophiques sur les preuves du Christianisme*, chap. xiii.

he may be in medical science, knows that certain things preserve health, while others destroy it, and if certainty were impossible without complete knowledge of the subject-matter, then science itself would perish, for any effect perceived might be attributed to some hitherto unknown cause.

Thus also is it as regards evidence of the supernatural. It is indeed impossible to determine how far the imagination influences the body, but we do know that it cannot give sight to the blind, nor hearing to one born deaf. We cannot gauge the limits of the inventiveness of man, or his control of the elements; but we do know that, unaided, he cannot ascend to the heavens, walk upon the waters, still the tempest by a word, or pass through closed doors. How long a death-like trance may last may be undeterminable, but we are certain that no mere natural power can call back the dead to life. Without this certainty, all rights, property, possessions, all family life, which are based on this conviction, would cease to be possible; for any man endowed with natural powers, supreme and occult such as those, would be master of the fate of his fellows, and the order of nature, thus alterable at the human will, would cease to exist.

A few words will suffice to explain the significance of prophecy. Prophecy is the certain prescience and prediction of a future event, absolutely imperceptible in any natural cause. Such a power, therefore, can only proceed from an Omniscient Being, independent of space and time; and its exercise has been ever regarded as a divine gift. As the organ of Revelation, prophecy shows how, amidst all the changes of human affairs, the plan of Redemption will be accomplished; and its fulfilment in the present and past stamps its authenticity, while it inspires the faith and hope of the believer in its predictions for the future.

The liberation of Israel, foretold by Moses, was in its accomplishment a sign of his divine mission; the prophets in their turn pointed to the fulfilment of their predictions as evidence that they spoke in the name of God;[1] and our Lord appealed both to the prophecies of the Old Testament,[2] and to His own, in proof of the truth of His word. "I have told you before it come to pass, that when it is come to pass, ye might believe."[3]

False religions have also claimed to possess His power. The Pagan world had its Soothsayers, Augurs, Oracles, Diviners; and the modern Theosophists and Spiritualists their mediums and clairvoyants. We must then, as with miracles, distinguish true prophecies from the false. First, as regards false prophecies. A large allowance must be made for the imposition and legerdemain of the operators and their confederates, and for the credulity and superstition of their hearers. Few oracles or mediums have ever been subjected to the same tests as ordinary conjurers. Secondly, most of their utterances are vague and indefinite sayings, pointless platitudes or sententious moral maxims.

---

[1] 1 Kings ii. 34; Isa. vii. 11; xxxvii. 7.
[2] John v. 39. [3] John xiii. 19; xiv. 29.

The answers given at Delphi consisted at first only of exhortations to amendment of life, and hence their high reputation with Socrates and Plato. When the oracle began to speak of the future, it became more and more obscure, till its ambiguity was proverbial. The answers of modern Spiritualists are of the same character. Thirdly, the oracle or the medium, before replying, was reduced to a state of unconsciousness or coma, and was in a wholly unhealthy and abnormal condition.

Women were preferred as Priestesses or Prophetesses, while the Prophets of the Bible are almost exclusively men. The Pythia inhaled the intoxicating vapours that rose from the spring at Delphi, chewed the narcotic laurel berry, and drank of the Castalian spring. In Hysiæ and Claros the Augurs were wont to drink intoxicating waters, and in Argos the blood of the sacrifices.

Virgil thus describes the frenzied condition of the Sybil, when about to deliver her responses:—

> "Her colour changed; her face was not the same;
> And hollow groans from her deep spirit came.
> Her hair stood up; convulsive rage possessed
> Her trembling limbs, and heaved her labouring breast.
> Greater than human kind she seemed to look;
> And with an accent more than mortal spoke:
> Her staring eyes with sparkling fury roll;
> When all the god came rushing on her soul.
> Swiftly she turned, and, foaming as she spoke:
> 'Why this delay? (she cried) the powers invoke!'"[1]

---

[1] Dryden, *Æneid*, vi. 72–81.

The modern medium is hypnotised or thrown into a magnetic or mesmeric trance. Now, the result of such nervous derangement is that the patient is peculiarly subject to atmospheric influence of all kinds ; and, just as sick persons can anticipate and foretell changes of temperature, of which those in health are wholly unconscious, though acted on by the same influences, so it is possible that any truth in the predictions of the mediums or oracles is partly due to the increased susceptibility of their hypnotised and nervous condition. Birds and animals instinctively recognise coming changes of weather long before men can do so, because the former, being irrational, are wholly subject to the impressions of sensible agents ; and it is not an absurd supposition that human beings, when artificially deprived of reason, may become, like the brutes, abnormally sensitive, and thus conscious of effects which their intellectual activity would screen from them.

For the rest, it may be said that any correct answer from such sources, not explicable by natural causes, can result only from diabolic intervention. St. Paul exorcised the girl with the Pythonical Spirit,[1] and the Fathers recount that the oracles spoke with difficulty in the presence of Christians.[2] The oracle of Apollo at Daphne was silenced as long as the body of the martyr Babylas lay near the spot; and hence its removal was peremptorily commanded by the apostate Julian.[3] The practice of divination or sooth-

---

[1] Acts xvi. 16.   [2] Lact., *Instit. Div.*, iv. 17.
[3] Socrat., *Hist. Eccles.*, iii. 18.

saying, in any form, has been repeatedly condemned by the Church, because it is against the honour due to God to attempt to obtain from any creature knowledge which is necessarily His alone; and therefore the attempt is equally sinful whether it succeed or not.

Compare with the condition and utterances of the false oracles and mediums those of the prophets endowed with the Spirit of God. First, instead of rendering himself unconscious or abnormally excited, the Prophet prepared himself for his task by solitude, fast, and prayer. Secondly, what they said was clear and definite; for example, the details they give as to the date, birthplace, life, and death of the Messias, and our Lord's own prophecies of His death, resurrection, and the destruction of Jerusalem. Lastly, they identified themselves with their words, lived and died in defence of their truth, and were thus the champions and martyrs of the people of God.

By miracles and prophecies then, as external patent signs of supernatural knowledge and power, the fact that God has spoken is announced plainly and most certainly to all men, whether simple or learned, and the refusal to recognise them erects an insuperable barrier between the soul and its God.

In conclusion, it is said, why does not God work one patent, indubitable miracle, and so convert thousands? Such an utterance is alike unreasonable, irreligious, and untrue. It is unreasonable, because miracles and prophecies are essentially extraordinary operations of divine power and wisdom; did they occur daily, and at all times and places, at the caprice of any who demanded them, they would cease to be miracles. And for the same reason prophecies are infrequent, because they would interfere with history and destroy the spontaneity and merit of human action. "If God," says Pascal, "were perpetually manifesting Himself to men, there would no longer be any merit in faith. And if He never manifested Himself, faith would be impossible."[1]

The demand for an undoubted miracle is also irreligious, for it assumes man's right to impose conditions upon his Creator, and is, indeed, a presumptuous challenge of God's power. It is the language of the tempter in the wilderness, "If Thou be the Son of God, command that these stones be made bread," or of the multitude on Calvary, "If Thou be the Son of God, come down from the Cross." Such language is also untrue, for where the will to believe is wanting no miracle will compel the assent. However great the wonder worked, the sceptic has a thousand excuses ready—inaccuracy in the reported fact, or illusion of sight or sense, or the intervention of some cause not known. "If I were to witness a resurrection," says Rousseau, "however astonished I might be, I cannot say what might happen. I should be more likely to go out of my mind than to believe,"[2] a remarkable illustration of the truth of the words, "They have Moses and the Prophets, if they hear not

[1] *Pensées*, ii. art. 16.   [2] *Ad. loc. cit.*

them, neither will they believe if one rose from the dead."[1] However great, then, the privilege enjoyed by our Lord's contemporaries of seeing Him face to face, yet we have in the accomplishment of prophecy evidence of His Divinity which was concealed from them; we see what they did not. "The whole Christ," says St. Augustine, "was revealed to the Apostles, and is also revealed to us, but He was not fully seen by them, nor is He fully seen by us. They saw the Head, and believed in the Body (the Church); we see the Body, and believe in the Head. The foundation and stability of the Church throughout the storms of past ages is a great and perpetual miracle visible to all the world, and the fulfilment of all prophecy."[2] This abiding miracle, indeed, confirms the truth of all others, and on evidence so strong and manifest that, as Bossuet has said, "What is hard to understand is, not the sublime mysteries proposed for our belief, but the blindness of those who refuse to receive them."[3]

[1] Luke xvi. 29, 31.   [2] Serm. cxvi. *Cf.* Serm. ccxlii.
[3] *Hist. Univ.*, ii.

CHAPTER IV

CREDIBILITY OF THE GOSPELS

SOPHISTICAL and fallacious arguments may distort or disguise truth, but history, the calm record of the past, is like the law of nature, unaffected by the passions and prejudices of man. Like Nature, again, it is the work of God, as accomplished by second causes, necessary and free ; and its pages reveal theories and facts in their true character and relation, and in their effects for good or evil. What, then, is the verdict of history as regards Christianity ? An unbiassed examination of the past shows, we maintain, that the person, life, and teaching of Christ are all strictly historic, and further, that His doctrine is so bound up with external events, that unless their truth be admitted, the record of the past is an enigma. Let us then, first, consider the testimony of universal history ; secondly, of non-christian historians ; thirdly, the credibility of the Gospel narratives themselves ; and lastly, the objections raised in ancient and modern times against their truth.

First, then, independent evidence of the facts related in the Gospel is found in the vast transformation, political, social, and religious, inaugurated during the period of only seventy years which the inspired records embrace. "This mere span of time is both the most marked and the most important in the history of the world. The foundation of the Christian Church closes a preparation of many thousand years, and inaugurates a new order of things—the world before and the world after Christ. Such is, and ever has been, the truest and simplest division of history."[1]

The universal change effected by Christianity in the heathen world, then, is a fact beyond dispute. We have already considered in Chapters I. and II.[2] how all that is best and highest in our actual civilisation is the product of Christian teaching; and the adaptability of its principles to every change in human thought and life, not opposed to the eternal law of God, is manifested afresh in each successive age. No Greek or Roman, however acute or impartial his judgment of the Infant Church might be, could ever have foreseen its future influence and power. Nay more, the Christians themselves, says Dr. Dollinger,[3] were far from appreciating the reach and the force for the world's culture of those spiritual and divine powers laid up in the bosom of their society, and entrusted to them and their administration. On the other hand, nearly 2000 years of Christian history are spread before our eyes, and in this long retrospect revelation, though once delivered in its fulness, is ever a new message from God to man. In its historical and external develop-

---

[1] Dollinger, *First Age of the Church*, Preface.
[2] Chap. i. p. 41 ; chap. ii. *passim*.
[3] Dollinger, *First Age of the Church*.

ment, in the power it continuously exercised of expressing precisely, in human terms, the deepest mysteries of faith, and its victorious conflict with error, the Church of Christ is ever making further advance and reaffirming its divine origin. Christianity, then, is an external fact, and its rise is inexplicable, save by the events recorded in the Gospel, and this is our first and independent witness to their credibility. Take away the Christian Christ and there is a blank in history.

Next let us consider the evidence of Pagan writers. The great events in Palestine, at Jerusalem, on Calvary, have been described by the chief historians of the ancient world, who have proclaimed through all time, in the Latin, Greek, and Hebrew tongues, like the threefold superscription on the Cross, the kingdom of Christ upon earth.

First Tacitus, the greatest of Roman historians, gives in his Annals the whole history of Christ, and he details concisely and forcibly names, places, and years, with the precision of a state document. He relates that in A.D. 64, barely thirty years after the death of our Lord, Nero set fire to Rome, that from the flames of the burning city he might picture to himself the fall of Troy. To divert suspicion from himself, he accused the Christians of being the incendiaries. "The public voice," Tacitus says, "having accused Nero of having commanded the burning of the city, in order to put an end to these rumours, he saddled the guilt on others, and punished with exquisite tortures those men, commonly called Christians, who were hated on account of their disgraceful actions. This name had its origin from Christ, who in the reign of Tiberius was executed by the governor Pontius Pilate. This deadly superstition, repressed for a moment, broke out afresh, not only in Judæa, where the evil first arose, but also in Rome itself. At first those only who confessed that they were Christians were incriminated, but afterwards, upon judicial inquiries, an immense number of persons were apprehended, not so much because they were the authors of the fire, but because they were hated by the whole human race." [1]

Thus the pagan historian confirms the words of the creed, " Suffered under Pontius Pilate," and only thirty years after the death of Christ in Rome itself Christians had so multiplied, that he could describe them as an immense multitude, even as compared with the teeming population of the imperial city. "The faith was, indeed, spoken of in the whole world." [2] Like a mighty stream the new doctrine burst through all barriers, the habits and usages of its disciples, so much opposed to those of the degenerate Romans, stimulating alike their curiosity and their hate.

Almost a contemporary of Tacitus is Suetonius. He confirms the account of Tacitus, and relates the fact of a tumultuous rising of the Jews about Christ,

---

[1] Tacitus, *Annal.*, xv. 38-44. *Cf.* Ruinart, *Act. Sincer. M. M. Præfat. general*, ii. 26, who quotes this passage against Dodwell (*De paucit M. M.*).

[2] Rom. i. 8.

and their consequent banishment from Rome by the Emperor Claudius about the year 20 A.D.

But who was this Christ, according to the belief of His followers? Was He, like Socrates, the founder of a school of philosophy, or a Jewish Rabbi like Hillel? We find an answer in a report furnished twenty years after the death of Christ by Pliny, viceroy of Bithynia, to his friend the Emperor Trajan, in which he gives the result of his judicial examination of the Christians. "They confessed," he says, "that they used to assemble together before dawn to sing praises to Christ as their God, and that they bound themselves by oath not to commit any crime, theft, adultery, or betrayal of trust. . . . Deeming it necessary to obtain fuller information of the truth, I caused some maidens, who were called servants (ministræ), to be apprehended and put on the rack, but I discovered nothing beyond an extravagant and degrading superstition. Seeing, however, the number of its followers, I have thought it expedient to have your opinion on the subject, for members of very high rank and either sex are imperilled by it. Towns, villages, and countries are infected on all sides by this superstition. The temples of the gods are almost deserted, and sacrifices are scarcely ever offered."[1]

Objection has been taken to these heathen accounts because of their brevity. But it must be remembered that the national and religious prejudice of the writers prevented any fuller investigation on their part of the

[1] Epp., l. x. 97.

new religion. Christians were in their eyes but one of the many ephemeral sects which were constantly appearing. But this same prejudice enhances the value of their evidence as coming from a pagan source. Of Christian witnesses there were more than sufficient. Tertullian says, "We were not born Christians, but have become so." And every Christian, such as the martyrs and confessors of the first ages, witnessed to the power of that truth for which he renounced all, and life itself.

Let us now turn to the East. Josephus Flavius was born three years after Christ. A Jew by descent and religion, but in education and habits of mind a Greek, he wrote the history of the Jewish people. In it he mentions John the Baptist,[1] his preaching, virtues, and violent death; he speaks of St. James the Apostle, whom he calls a brother of Jesus, "who was called Christ,"[2] and of Him he thus writes: "At that time lived Jesus, a wise man, if He is to be called a man, for His works were marvellous; a teacher of those who hear the truth with gladness. He had many disciples, who followed Him, both among the Jews and the Greeks. This was the Christ. Pilate, on the accusation of the chief men amongst us, caused Him to be crucified. But this did not hinder His disciples from continuing to love Him as before. He appeared to them alive, three days after His death, for the divine prophets had foretold this miracle and many other wonderful things, and this people of

[1] *Antiquit. Jud.*, xviii. 5, 2.   [2] L. C. xx. 9, 1.

Christians still continue to be called after Him."[1] In modern times the genuineness of this passage has been disputed; but Eusebius[2] makes mention of it, whilst Sozomen,[3] Isidore of Pelusium,[4] and Rufinius[5] refer to it. Josephus could not omit a mention of Christ, for he was giving an account of all the sects and party leaders among the Jews, from Augustus to the destruction of Jerusalem. If the passage is an interpolation, it can only be regarded as such on the inconceivable suggestion that all the copies of his work were in Christian, not one in Jewish or heathen hands. Such laudatory language concerning Christ from an unbeliever in Him, is explained by the fact that Josephus, as an historian of Hellenistic and somewhat eclectic tendencies, simply relates what he heard of Christ, and what His disciples held about Him. St. Jerome, therefore, rightly translates Ὁ Χριστὸς οὗτος ἦν,[6] "Credebatur esse Christus." Justin and Tertullian do not quote his testimony, because his history, being written in the interest of the Romans, was especially odious to the Jews.

But the Jews themselves bear witness in their Talmud to Christ, His wonders and His death. The Talmud ranks next to the Sacred Scriptures with the Jewish people, as it contains their authentic traditions and teachings from the earliest to the first Christian times. One of its treatises, entitled "Sanhedrin," gives

---

[1] *Antiquit. Jud.*, xviii. 3, 3.
[2] H. E., i. 11.
[3] H. E., i. 1.
[4] *Epist.*, iv. 225.
[5] H. E., iii. 1.
[6] *De Scriptor. Eccles.*, c. xiii.

the following statement. "Christ," it says, "was put to death on the Eve of Easter, because He had practised enchantments (the Beelzebub of the Gospel narrator), and perverted the people of Israel, and led them to embrace a strange religion. As no defence could be found for this, He was crucified on the Eve of the Pasch." According to the Talmud, again, He had learnt magic in Egypt,[1] and thence brought magical arts—incisions made in His flesh—by which He worked miracles, and misled the people to believe that He wrought them by His own power. Thus Romans, Greeks, and Jews are witnesses of Christ, and all history is the great commentary on the simple Gospel narrative. A man despised and crucified is the Founder of a great community, which with unshaken faith maintains His Divinity against both Jew and heathen persecution.

Finally, the narratives of the four Evangelists prove the historic truth of the life of Christ. Not that Christianity rests only upon belief in the Sacred Scriptures, or would perish in their destruction. For Christianity is ever living in the Church, and her divine self-consciousness, or tradition, ever witnesses to its truth. Still the Gospel records, though not Christ Himself, but only the inspired testimony to His Divinity, are our most precious possession. Written in diverse places, they bear traces of their origin. Their language is a Greek idiom, which represents the fusion of the East and West, of the

[1] *Sanhed.*, fol. 107.

Israelite with the heathen, the entering, as it were, of Japhet into the tents of Sem. They include every variety of writing, historic and epistolary, culminating in the prophecy of the Apocalypse. Though deficient in much that we admire in classical, oriental, or modern works, they possess a noble simplicity and unobtrusive grandeur, a supernatural beauty all their own. Their authors, for the most part, passed amongst their fellow-countrymen for simple unlearned men; yet how irresistible the charm, how inexhaustible the depth, how perfect the design of their composition. Although written chiefly for some special purpose, yet their significance is lasting, their style simple and yet elevated, their language, even when provincial and childish, always beautiful and stately. We may be at times startled, if not scandalised, yet in the end they triumph over all our doubts and cavils.[1]

Now, are these narratives genuine? that is, are they indeed written by those whose names they bear? The primary witness for the genuineness of the Gospels is the Church, for they were written within her fold, and compiled for her use. Hence the evidence in their behalf is of a very special kind. Unlike ordinary books that are written for private and unknown readers, who have no interest in their preservation, the Gospels were composed by the Apostles themselves, or under their direction, as official documents for the use of the churches they had founded. These churches were great public, exclusive, autonomous

[1] *Cf.* Delitzch, *Apolog.*, p. 442.

communities, with their own tribunals and rulers, with one common creed and close intercommunion. It was in the midst of these churches that the Gospels first appeared, and were ever after treasured as the Magna Charta, the title-deeds of their faith. The authenticity of the Gospels was guaranteed in the first instance by the Bishops, who received them directly from their authors, and gave them their titles indicative of their nation and authorship. The authoritative character of these titles appear, from the charge brought by Tertullian against the heretic Marcion, of changing the title of the Epistle to the Ephesians, which "*the Church alone could fix.*" It was indeed necessary that these books should be officially recognised and distinguished, for their reading formed an essential part in the divine services, and "caused," as Tertullian says, "the voices of the Apostles to be heard anew, and their countenances to be again seen." This public liturgical use of the sacred books served further as one great means of protecting the text from any innovation or change.

We will now give a summary of the chief patristic authorities for the four Gospels. First in order of time are the writings of the Apostolic Fathers, A.D. 70–120; St. Clement of Rome, A.D. 101; St. Ignatius, Bishop of Antioch, A.D. 107; St. Polycarp, A.D. 112; the author of the Epistle of Barnabas about A.D. 80. These writers give passages substantially in agreement with our present Gospels, and though they do not cite an Evangelist by name, this need not surprise us, for they quote the Old Testament in the same way, without mentioning the author referred to. The next period, A.D. 120–170, supplies evidence not only for the existence of the Gospels, but also for their number and authorship. St. Justin, in his Apology, which must have been compiled between A.D. 138 and 160, tells us, in his description of the Eucharistic feast, " that the memoirs of the Apostles that are called Gospels are publicly read together with the writings of the prophets in the assemblies of the Christians."[1] In his dialogue with Trypho, he says that these memoirs were written by the Apostles themselves and by their disciples. Thus he recognises two Gospels at least as the works of the Apostles and two of their disciples, a distinction corresponding to the present Gospel Canon. As Justin was converted about A.D. 130, and he speaks of what was already an established custom, it is evident that at the commencement of the second century, whilst the disciples of the Apostles were still living, the Gospels were universally recognised as the composition of the Apostles, and formed as definite a collection of writing as the prophetic books of the Old Testament, and held equal rank with them. Papias, Bishop of Hierapolis, A.D. 140, an associate of the immediate disciples of the Apostles, probably used the four Gospels, and speaks of St. Matthew and St. Mark by name, and says that Matthew wrote the oracles (λογία) [of the Lord], in the Hebrew

[1] *Apolog.*, i. 67.

language, and "that Mark did not write the words or deeds of Christ in order" (of time).[1] Tatian's Diatessaron, composed about 150 A.D., contains the *four* Gospels entire, with the exception of the genealogies, and is a witness of supreme importance, as showing again the exclusive authority enjoyed by these documents as early as the middle of the second century. The Muratori Canon, probably compiled at Rome about 170 A.D., gives a nearly complete list of the New Testament writings, and is herein supported and supplemented by the Peschito or the Syriac version in the East.

In the third period, from A.D. 170 to the close of the second century, Tertullian writes as the representative of the Latin speaking portion of the Roman Church. Though now a Montanist, he defends the New Testament against the heretic Marcion, and regards the authenticity of the four Gospels as undoubted.[2] St. Clement of Alexandria, A.D. 180, distinguishes the four canonical Gospels from the apocryphal one "according to the Egyptians," and speaks of them as those that "have been delivered to us."[3]

St. Irenæus, A.D. 180, who, when a youth, sat at the feet of St. Polycarp,[4] himself a disciple of the Apostles, tells us that the four Gospels had long been known and read in the Church, and venerated as an heritage and legacy from the Apostles. These witnesses, be it observed, speak officially as Bishops,

---

[1] Euseb., H. E., iii. 39. [2] C. Marcion, iv. 35; v. 17.
[3] Strom., iii. 13, i. 21. [4] Euseb., H. E., v. 20.

and as the appointed guardians of the universal consciousness of the Church and of her immemorial traditions.[1]

Finally, various early versions fix for us again the date of the Gospels. Tertullian employed the old Latin version (Itala), probably of African origin, and which was in use in the second century. According to the tradition of the Church of Syria, the Syriac translation, the Peschito, is coeval with the preaching of Christianity in the Aramaic regions, and especially in Edessa. Hegisippus appeals to the Syriac Gospel.[2]

External corroborative evidence to the authenticity of the Gospels is found in the writings of the heresiarchs of the second century. Chief of these are Basilides, a disciple of Simon Magus, and Valentinus, Gnostic teachers who are both mentioned by St. Justin, and must therefore have lived in the first half of the second century. Both these writers make use of the Gospels, and particularly of St. John's, thus showing the early date at which it was held in honour outside the Church. Nor is its rejection by individuals like Cerinthius any counter-argument, for their refusal to accept it was based, like that of the

---

[1] St. Irenæus argues in favour of the long established four Gospels upon grounds of congruity. As there are four quarters of the globe, four beasts in the Apocalypse, so there are four Gospels; and in this symbolism he finds evidence for their unity, universality, dignity, and necessity.

[2] Euseb., H. E., iv. 30; Wichelhaus, *De N. T. versione, Syriac,* 150; *cf.* Haneburg, *loc. cit.,* p. 66 ff.

Ebionites with regard to St. Matthew's Gospel, purely on dogmatic grounds, and not from any doubt as to its authenticity.

Another proof of the genuineness of the Gospels is found in the jealous care with which the Church watched over the apostolical traditions, ordinances, and above all, the sacred writings. When the Church of Philippi desired to form a collection of the Epistles of St. Ignatius, in order to secure a faithful copy, they applied to his friend Polycarp, a disciple of the Apostle St. John. When the Paschal controversy broke out, as to whether Easter should be kept on the fourteenth Nizam with the Eastern Church, or with the Western, on the following Sunday, St. Polycarp, then a very old man, repaired (162 A.D.) to settle the question with Anicetus, Bishop of Rome, by ascertaining the apostolic tradition on this point. All attempts to tamper with the traditions of the faith were instantly repelled. St. John left the bath-house at Ephesus, because Cerinthius the heretic had entered it, and he forbids the faithful to say " God speed thee " to a heretic. St. Ignatius is equally firm. He calls strange doctrine "a poisonous plant," and gives repeated warnings against intercourse with heretical teachers.[1] St. Polycarp's reply to Marcion, "I know thee, thou first-born of Satan,"[2] testifies to the insuperable barrier raised by the Church against the assaults of error. Hegesippus, a Jew by birth, A.D. 150, tells us that in his first journey from the East to Rome,

[1] Trall, a. vi. ; Smyrna, c. vi.   [2] Euseb., H. E., iv. 21.

he had confidential intercourse with many Bishops, and found that all taught the same doctrine. This statement is the more valuable, because, on the one hand, he was cognisant of the whole course of Gnosticism, from Simon Magus down to his own contemporaries, Marcion and Valentinus; and on the other, his intercourse with Pope Anicetus enabled him to compare the dogmatic teaching of the East with that of the West.[1] The fifty-ninth Apostolic Canon anathematises every one who presumes to propagate apocryphal writings in the Church.[2] According to St. Augustine,[3] the high esteem in which the Gospels were held in the Church was primarily due to the fact, "that she received them from the hands of the Apostles themselves, to whose preaching she owed her faith and her very existence."

To sum up. The universal spread of the Gospels, the close union between the churches, the public supervision secured by their liturgical use, the scrupulous care employed in preserving the apostolic traditions, the brief period that elapsed between their compilation during the lifetime of the Apostles and their contemporaries, and their universal acceptance in the churches, prove beyond doubt the authenticity of these documents, unless scepticism be carried to an extent destructive of all history. Further, the witnesses to the historic truth of the Gospels form a class apart.

---

[1] *Cf.* D. Haneberg, Renan's *Leben Jesu beleuchtet*, Munich, 1854. pp. 63–65.
[2] *Potr. Apost. ap. Cotel*, i. p. 445. [3] *Ep.* lxxxii. 7 *ad Hieron.*

They gave their evidence at the cost of severe self-sacrifice and suffering, often of life itself. For what other books have such torrents of blood been shed!

Again, the Gospels themselves contain intrinsic evidence of the strongest kind for their genuineness and credibility. Wherever we open their pages, we find an originality of thought, a simplicity and purity, an absence of all egotism without parallel! The writers narrate, without any expression of amazement, astounding facts, such as the raising of the dead to life. They recount their own sins, weaknesses, and follies, yet never excuse themselves. They narrate the treason of Judas, the cowardice of Pilate, and no word of reproach escapes their pen. They tell again of the insults heaped upon Christ, the calumnious accusations made against their beloved Master, without attempting His defence. Every word bears the stamp of personal experience; the minute and lucid details, the trifling incidents, the dramatic freshness and intuition, especially in the fourth Gospel, could only have emanated from eye-witnesses of the events.[1]

The first words of St. John's Gospel, "In the beginning was the Word," are instinct with the most sublime and elevated thought, more proper to Heaven than earth. Suddenly the tone changes, as with

---

[1] For instance, John xx. 25; Luke xxii. 41. "He was withdrawn from them a stone's cast, and while He was yet speaking, behold" (Mark xiv. 43). "And one of them struck the servant of the High Priest, and cut off his right ear" (Luke xxii. 50). The distance of space, the concurrence in time, the special member healed, herein recorded, would never have been invented by a forger.

childlike devotion the disciple speaks of his beloved Master by His sacred human name, and by the shepherd's title as the Lamb of God. How vividly each group stands out! St. John has followed every footstep, has known each individual character. How modestly he mentions his nameless self, yet continually repeats "what we ourselves have seen." From the very first chapters the conviction is irresistible that the writer speaks from his own consciousness, and, even after the lapse of 1800 years, that the language is that of truth, and of truth at first hand.

And there is every reason why this should be so. Our Lord's companions throughout His three years' ministry—the Evangelists and Apostles, the seventy-two disciples—were clearly competent to describe truthfully the events they had witnessed. These events had taken place in public, many of them had been subjected to hostile investigation, and all of them could be verified by every man possessed of his senses. Besides, far from being credulous, the disciples were strangely indisposed to believe.[1] One of them was only convinced by actually touching the sacred wounds.

Had they intended to deceive, they would have written in concert, and have carefully excluded the apparent discrepancies in their narratives. On the other hand, as independent, merely human writers, their essential agreement both as to facts and doc-

[1] *Cf.* Mark xvi. 11 ; Luke xxiv. 41 ; Matt. xxviii. 17 ; John xx. 25.

trines is truly marvellous. "Consider," says even Rousseau, "the gentleness of Jesus, the purity of His morals, the persuasiveness of His teaching. How lofty His principles! what wisdom in His words! how opportune, frank, and direct His answers! How can the Gospel history be an invention? My friend, forgeries are not of this kind; and the acts of Socrates, which no one doubts, are not so well attested as the acts of Christ. Besides, this only increases the difficulty. Far more inconceivable is it that several men should have combined to fabricate this book than that there should have been one living original whom they described. No Jewish author could have fabricated the tone or the moral teaching of the Evangelist. So powerful, overwhelming, and inimitable is the impress of truth stamped upon the Gospel, that its inventor would be a greater marvel than its hero!"[1]

"Now, this has often appeared to me," says Cardinal Wiseman, "the strongest internal proof of a superior authority stamped upon the Gospel history, that the holy and perfect character it portrays not only differs from, but expressly opposes, every type of moral perfection which they who wrote it could possibly have conceived. We have in the writings of the Rabbis ample materials wherewith to construct the model of a perfect Jewish teacher. We have the sayings and the actions of Hillel and Gamaliel and Rabbi Samuel, all perhaps in great part imaginary, but all bearing

[1] Rousseau, *Emile*, iv.

the impress of national ideas, all formed upon one
rule of imaginary perfection. Yet nothing can be
more widely apart than their thoughts and principles
of actions and character and those of our Redeemer.
Lovers of wrangling controversy, proposers of captious
paradoxes, jealous upholders of their nation's exclusive privileges, uncompromising sticklers for the least
comma of the Law, and most sophistical departers from
its spirit, such mostly are these great men, the exact
counterpart and reflection of those Scribes and Pharisees who are so uncompromisingly reproved as the
very contradiction of Gospel principles. How comes
it that men, not even learned, contrived to represent
a character every way departing from their national
type, at variance with all those features which custom,
education, patriotism, religion, and nature alike, seemed
to have consecrated as of all most beautiful? And
the difficulty of considering such a character the invention of man . . . is still further increased by observing
how writers recording different facts, as St. Matthew
and St. John, do lead us, nevertheless, to the same
representation and conception. Yet herein, methinks,
we have a key to the solution of every difficulty. . . .
The Evangelists must have copied the living Model
which they represent; and the accordance of the moral
features which they give Him can only proceed from
the accuracy with which they have respectively drawn
them." [1]

[1] *Science and Revealed Religion*, Lect. IV.; *Dublin Review*, 1866,
p. 175.

Renan himself unwittingly confirms the Cardinal's words by showing the kind of portrait which a vain, fanciful imagination can draw of the Founder of Christianity. Professedly a work of great learning, but without depth or originality either of thought or research, his " Vie de Jesus " sees in Christ " le jeune Democrat," and recasts the Gospel history on the lines of a sentimental French society novel. What is original in his work is founded totally on his own conjectures, unsupported by any kind of authority. He speaks of " sisters of Jesus," married in Nazareth; of the "children of St. Peter; " and tells us that Jesus used often to ride upon an ass, upon which His disciples were accustomed to spread their garments; that Judas *probably* lived quietly in his cottage on the field of Aceldama; that St. John wrote his Gospel because he was piqued at the pre-eminence given to St. Peter in the other Gospels. Finally, he shows his critical judgment by characterising the sublime discourse, as even De Witte acknowledges it to be, in John xvii., as " rhétorique, vain et fastidieux apprêt."

But to return to the Gospels. Only those who had witnessed Christ's life could write His history. At the time of our Lord's advent, and in the century before and after Him, Jewish, Greek, and Roman nationalities and manners were intermingled with their threefold language and perpetually changing governments; Judea, the scene and theatre of the Gospel history, was, shortly after the ascension of Christ, utterly desolated and revolutionised. Under such circumstances, how difficult it would have been, for other than eye-witnesses, to avoid misrepresentations and mistakes. Yet not a single detail in the Gospel history contradicts any circumstance of time, place, or persons. The attacks of hostile criticism during well nigh two thousand years have only confirmed the accuracy of the Evangelists. For example, the insidious question concerning the tribute [1] imposed by Cæsar on the Jews, fixes the date of our Lord's life; for only during a short period was that tribute levied. We find mention of Greek, Roman, and Jewish coins; the customs were paid in Greek money; the sanctuary offerings in the old national coinage; while the Roman denarii and asses were current for daily use. Places are spoken of by the names by which they were known at that precise time, although thirty years earlier or later they often bore different appellations. For instance, Sichem, Flavia or Mabortha, Cæsarea, Paneas, Philippi.

Had the New Testament been a forgery, in no book ever compiled would the deception have been so easily detected. The scene of action is not confined to one country, but extends to the most important cities of the Roman Empire. We find allusions to the customs and ideas of Greeks and Romans; and as to the Jews, these allusions include even the absurdities and follies of their schools. Whatever familiarity with the classic authors a Greek or Roman

[1] Mark xii. 14: "Is it lawful to give tribute to Cæsar; or shall we not give it?"

Christian of the second century possessed, he would be less versed in Jewish literature; and a Jewish convert, even if a learned Rabbi, would have known little of that of Greece or Rome.[1]

"Most students of ancient manuscripts," says Haneberg, "must have remarked their paucity of geographical details, their inveracity in topographical statements, according as they are non-historic or the reverse. Topographical data are characteristic of works written by eye-witnesses, or compiled from reliable sources. Xenophon's Anabasis is a very repertory for the geographer, while his Cyropædia is poor in local designations. The pseudo Vakidi's work on the conquest of Syria leaves us in the dark as to the early migrations of the Arabs. How scanty are the topographical details of the Gnostic work Pistis-sophia! whilst the Apocryphal Gospels are, as regards geography, a blank. Far otherwise is it with the Canonical Gospels. Only eye-witnesses could have given us details so precise as, *e.g.*, those in the fourth Gospel on the destruction of Jerusalem, A.D. 70."[2]

This internal evidence for the truth of the Gospels may well suffice, but we will add a few remarks. Suppose, then, a great historic event to have taken place, a revolution which decided the fate of a nation, and that it was witnessed by a man of education and learning, by profession a physician, who undertook to

---

[1] *Cf.* Michaelis, *Einleitung in das II. Testament.*
[2] Renan, *Leben Jesu beleuchtet*, p. 31.

relate its history. Further, that for this purpose he arranges and classifies events, separates what is false from the truth, admits nothing save on the testimony of eye-witnesses or actors in the occurrence, and then sends this carefully prepared account to a friend; would it be stigmatised, *primâ facie*, as a mass of errors and falsehoods, a mixture of fact and imagination? Yet it is precisely under these circumstances and with this motive that St. Luke, himself a learned physician, prepared, as he tells us, his Gospel.

His preamble [1] corresponds almost word for word with that of Thucydides, the father of critical history.[2] In the Acts of the Apostles, which is unquestionably St. Luke's writing, he refers to his Gospel (Acts i. 1), and alludes to its authorship as "the former treatise" which he had made "of all things which Jesus began to do and to teach." The Acts of the Apostles, especially in the second part, read like a traveller's journal, and show the historical accuracy of the third Evangelist. Again, St. John displays a love of historic truth, rare among biographers, by his careful contradiction of a false report which had got abroad from a misinterpreted saying of our Lord relative to St. Peter's death—" And Jesus did *not* say to him, He should not die: but, so I will have him to remain till I come, what is it to thee?"[3]

Next, a man of commanding intellect, strong will, intensely earnest in all his undertakings, learned in

---

[1] Luke i. 4.   [2] *De Bell. Pel.*, i. c. 22.
[3] John xxi. 22.

the literature of Greece and Judea, a prominent member of a powerful political religious party, finds himself confronted with a new teaching wholly antagonistic to his convictions and feelings, and he persecutes its disciples to the death. Suddenly he declares himself the avowed champion of the detested doctrine, and attributes his conversion to a vision manifested to him while actually engaged in his work of persecution. If his whole subsequent life shows no trace of mental aberration, or of fanatical delusion, but a marvellous clearness of thought and judgment, and a reverent love of truth; if he is ever impatient of superstition and credulity in any form, inveighs against "giving heed to foolish or old wives' fables,[1] and appeals against the inventions of false teachers to historic facts and the testimony of eye-witnesses, surely his evidence as to his conversion is worthy of credence, and the change from Saul the persecutor to Paul the Apostle is of itself a marvellous proof of the power of the religion which he embraced, and of its supernatural origin. And so complete is his testimony, that even without the Gospels, the truth of the leading facts of the life of Christ would be firmly established by those Epistles of St. Paul whose authenticity the most sceptical critics do not dispute.

Thus from every point of view the Gospels bear the stamp of authenticity, and as their characteristics are investigated, their truth becomes ever more apparent. We have now only to examine the

[1] 1 Tim. i. 4.

principles[1] on which modern sceptics reject the Gospels.

First among these is the assumption, or rather the series of assumptions, that miracles are impossible, and consequently the one, related by the Evangelists, which includes all others, *i.e.*, the miracle of the Incarnation, could never have occurred. Now, the impossibility of miracles assumes the non-existence of God; but as His existence is demonstrable, and cannot be disproved, trustworthy evidence of the occurrence of miracles, such as the Scriptures give, ought to be accepted; especially, as otherwise it is impossible to account for the new order of things, which still exists, and which began with these very miraculous events, related in the Gospel narrative.

But Strauss objects that as religion everywhere begins with myths, we may expect to find them in the commencement of Christianity. What then were the myths of Egypt and Greece? In these vague, unsubstantial fables, things of earth and heaven, history and fiction, God and matter, nature and spirit, moral freedom and physical necessity, are hopelessly intermingled and confused. So, too, the huge grotesque, sanguinary Indian idols, the shadowy German and Scandinavian deities, appear as phantom forms, half divine, half human, the creations of an imagination diseased, of man, the worshipper, and the slave of the material world. On the other hand, in Christ we see a

[1] The objections themselves are examined in the Appendix.

real intelligent, living Person, with a definite work and purpose, before which the dreams of Paganism vanish. Sages, like Plato, strove to employ the old world myths as a means of popularising their teaching, but in vain ; falsehood could not be the vehicle of truth. The facts of Revelation, on the other hand, prove themselves the very embodiment of the ideal, and in proportion as these facts are grasped is the ideal found to be realised therein. As regards the assertion of Strauss, the myth is no more the beginning of the religious consciousness in mankind than barbarism is the commencement of its civilisation, but are alike the results of falsehood, corruption, and decay.

Again, if Christianity had been nothing more than the highest development of humanity, why was it not recognised as such ? Why was it persecuted by the whole world, Greek, Roman, and Jewish ; high and low, civilised and barbarian ? Why did not men see that they were contending against their own highest ideal, their very flesh and blood ? Or if, as Baur says, the mythical Christ was invented by the Christian Community late in the second century, who founded that Community, which only existed through faith in Him ? The myth can neither form nor create ; it is an effect not a cause, the product of popular imagination in the infancy of a race. When we reflect on the Jews' expectation, at that time, of a victorious and world-wide ruler, and their consequent abhorrence of a crucified Messias, the fact of the foundation of the Christian Community amidst those very Jews, can only be explained by a second fact, the Divinity of Christ and the truth of His Resurrection.

Thirdly, according to Strauss, the pantheistic conception of the essential unity of the Godhead and Manhood, combined with the expectation of the Messias, gave rise to this "group of legends" which transferred to One, in the Person of Christ, as we see in the Gospels, what belonged to mankind as a whole. But this idea was not original; it had long existed under divers forms—for instance, among the neo-platonic schools of Greece, and in the Indian religions. If this was so, why then did the idea take form in Christianity alone? Why did it not find expression elsewhere? Merely human ideas, or rather the philosophers who conceived them, have founded schools in succession, but never an enduring world-wide Church. "The philosophers," says Voltaire, "never could persuade even those who lived in the same street with them." Doubtless we find in the best Jewish and Pagan writers precepts corresponding with those of the Gospel. But, apart from the primitive traditions which were by no means wholly lost, this only proves that Christianity contains all that is true and truly human in all religions.

"As to the theory of the mythical apotheosis of the life of Jesus," says Schelling, "every one will admit that no life has ever been transfigured by myths or legends, unless owing to previous great actions or other causes, it had already been idealised. The question then is, How came the Jewish Rabbi

Jesus to be the object of such an apotheosis? Was it on account of His teaching? But the stones which they cast at Him show their appreciation of His doctrines! Upon what supposition can we credit so marvellous a glorification? Since the immense majority of His nation certainly did not believe Him to be the Messias, it is only by admitting the truth of what Pagan and Old Testament writers, independently of the Gospels, affirm of the Person of Christ, that we can explain the origin of the dogmatic myth. But such an admission presupposes the greatness of Christ, independently of the Gospels. . . . We do not need the Gospels to attest His greatness; on the contrary, we must first admit His greatness, if we would understand the Gospel narrative."[1]

The Gospel history is no myth. Only in its infancy, as has been said, before the distinction between the domain of the imagination and that of fact has been realised, can a people, such as the Greeks or the Germans, create the dreams of its mythology, which always relate to the origin of the nation and its connection with the powers of nature therein personified. Myth appears before history and chronology, before documentary records; for writing, as Livy says, is the faithful guardian of the past. Thus, Theodoric has his epic, not Charlemagne; the heroes of Troy, not those of Marathon and Salamis.

Now the Gospels were written in an age of great

[1] *Philos. der Offenbarung*, v. ii. 4, p. 233.

intellectual activity, of unbelief and scepticism, when men like Cicero, as Plato before him, regarded the myth as a mere play of poetic imagination. It was a time also of historic criticism and literary activity. Thucydides was long since famous in Greece, Livy and Tacitus were writing in Rome, Josephus, and, a century previous, the Machabees in Judea, whilst the countries surrounding Judea, Egypt, Phenicia, and Chaldea, had each their local historians.

Manetho wrote the history of Egypt A.D. 263, Dios and Menander that of Phenicia, Ptolemy the Mendesian that of Herod, who himself was the author of Memoirs.[1] In such an age, credulity and superstition being, as has been said, the constant accompaniment of scepticism, there may be falsifications of history or conscious fiction, but not myths, which are the unconscious product of legend and poetry, "a substance," by the way, "as mysterious as the inspiration of the orthodox." So says Beuno Baur, a sceptical critic. In Rome and Alexandria and other cities there were public and private libraries, booksellers with offices for transcribers. One hundred scribes supplied five hundred copies of a book of Martial's poems in a single day; and there were reading rooms in the most frequented streets. Such was the age in which the Gospels appeared.

But this is not all. Myths are formed by a gradual process, extending over a long series of generations. Homer's epic appears two hundred years after the fall

[1] Hug., *Gutachten über das Leben Jesu von Strauss*, p. 50.

of Troy. But scarcely had one generation passed away after the death of Christ, before the Gospels were written, and towards the middle and end of the second century, we find them universally received in Gaul, Asia Minor, Alexandria, and Rome. We have already pointed out that this fact implies the existence of a common tradition, as otherwise it would be impossible to account for the universal acceptance of these four Gospels and none other, out of the mass of apocryphal writings. The Apostles lived until towards the end of the first century; indeed, St. John was still living at the time when, according to Pliny, Christianity had spread throughout Asia Minor.[1] What opportunity was there, then, for the formation of myths? Neither among Jews nor Christians were the Gospels discredited as forged fabrications; the evidence in their favour was too strong. Quadratus, a disciple of the Apostles, and, according to many authorities, Bishop of Athens, addressed in 126 A.D. an apology in favour of the Christians to the Emperor Adrian. The apology has perished, but the following remarkable passage has been preserved by Eusebius: "Our Saviour's works were enduring, for they were real. I appeal herewith to those who were healed by Him, to those He raised from the dead. They were seen, not only at the moment, when restored to health or recalled to life, but long after. They were still living during the life of our Lord and after His Ascension; some even survived to our own time."[2] The edict of the Emperor

---

[1] *Loc. cit.*   [2] *Hist. Eccles.*, iv. 3.

in favour of Christians was at least partly due to this apology.

But again, it is alleged that, setting aside all metaphysical and dogmatic difficulties, even apart from the miracles, still the Gospels contain so many contradictions, that it is impossible for a critical age to regard them as historic. On this point Pascal remarks: "What at first sight seems a weakness is, when rightly regarded, a proof of strength."[1] When St. John wrote his Gospel, he had the others before him; how was it, then, that he did not observe these contradictions? Doubtless there are in the Gospels various modes of representation; but these only prove the sincerity of the writers, to whom it never occurred that the truth of their accounts might be questioned. St. Luke gives three narratives of St. Paul's conversion,[2] and there are divergences in each. If these were real contradictions, surely he would have been the first to remark them! "Far from finding difficulties in the divergences in the four Gospels," says Salvador, a Jewish writer, "they are to my mind a priceless treasure, preserving, as they do, the unconscious and first impressions of the men and the events."[3]

The Gospels do not aim at being complete biographies of Christ; in each the history subserves one supreme end—to represent as concisely as possible the lifelike image of Christ. Hence, their words are chosen with

---

[1] *Pensées*, part iii. art. 13. [2] Acts ix. 15; xxii. 14; xxvi. 16.
[3] *Jesus Christ et sa doctrine*, l. ii. p. 67.

rare self-restraint, with simple, yet consummate art, and notwithstanding abridgments, breaks, and the absence of chronological order, are woven into one continuous whole. As a single sunbeam is refracted by the prism into manifold colours, so the One Infinite Person, Christ Jesus, is understood and drawn by the different Evangelists according to their individual characters, and for their special aims. "A different likeness," says Humboldt, "but always the truth." Plato and Xenophon paint Socrates under very different aspects, yet the philosopher stands before us as one and the same personality. "When," says Lessing, "Livy, Polybius, and Tacitus describe the same event with such diversities as to contradict each other, has the event itself, in which they all agree, ever been denied?"[1]

Our adversaries point to the great difference between the teaching of Jesus in the three first Gospels and in the fourth. But the reason is obvious. As the parables belong to the Galilean cycle of teaching, and represent the popular element in His preaching, and were easily intelligible, they naturally come first in the Synoptics. On the other hand, St. John portrays our Lord in His intercourse with the Scribes and Pharisees at Jerusalem. The discourses which he records had fixed themselves in his own recollection, and were not such as would have been retained by every hearer. And yet in both the Synoptics and St. John, the same ruling principle and spirit appears, the ascent from

[1] *Duplik.*

things visible and of earth to things spiritual and of heaven. The discourses recorded by St. John on the Bread of Life, the living Water, the good Shepherd, the true Vine, are in fullest harmony with the parables; while he repeats much of our Lord's teaching, especially the long discourses given in the Synoptics. Again, much stress is laid on the fact that our Lord is called in the Synoptics the Son of Man, in St. John the Son of God. Doubtless these two designations were adapted to the several purposes of our Lord's instructions, whether given to His disciples or to the multitude; but as regards His Person, there is the most perfect harmony. The Synoptics insist on the supremacy of His claims over every earthly tie;[1] attribute to Him omnipotence and omniscience in common with the Father;[2] and enforce the obligation of confessing Him as the condition of salvation.[3] Such prerogatives can only belong to the Divine Person described by St. John, in whom to believe is life everlasting;[4] Who is all holy,[5] and is One with the Father.[6] Indeed, this unanimity in all four Evangelists as to the Divinity of Christ, notwithstanding diversities of detail, is in the highest degree significant.

But false Gospels have existed—how can we be sure that ours are genuine? We reply—First, the apocryphal writings are distinguished by their dates, for most of them appeared in the fourth century,

[1] Matt. x. 37; Luke xiv. 26.
[2] Matt. xi. 27.
[3] Matt. x. 22; Mark viii. 38.
[4] John iii. 36.
[5] John viii. 46.
[6] John x. 30.

two centuries later than the true Gospels. Two of them, the Protoevangelium or the Gospel of James and the Acts of Pilate, were composed, according to many writers, at the beginning of the second century, and thus confirm the early date of the acceptance of the true Gospels by the Church. Secondly, they are distinguished by the heretical character of their doctrine, and by their frivolous and gossipy contents,[1] due to the fact that they were composed by Judaising and Gnostic sects, in order to claim our Lord's authority in support of their false teaching. Lastly, they are unable to show historic evidence in their favour, or that they ever possessed weight or authority in the Church.[2] These spurious documents serve, however, to establish the truth of the Canonical Gospels. Although the product of different authors, written in places and with views the most diverse, still all alike contain the essence of the Gospel history, the life and teaching of Christ, His miracles and Resurrection—in short, all that is of supreme importance.

To sum up. The sceptical thesis stands thus. Twelve Galilean fishermen devised the ideal Christ, and upon this imaginary basis reared the whole edifice of the Christian Church, and thus accomplished what Plato, Aristotle, or other philosophers never even conceived. This dream or myth has quickened and developed the mightiest intellects for nigh two

[1] Hug., *Gutachten über das Leben Jesu von Strauss*, p. 56.
[2] *Cf.* Eusebius, H. E., iii 29.

VITALITY OF THE GOSPELS

thousand years, has inspired millions to lead lives of self-sacrifice and suffering, and to shed their blood for its truth; and finally produced the whole system of civilisation on which the world's order rests. This same faith still quickens the Catholic Church, with all her marvellous institutions for every need of man, and gives her a vitality which, though ever assailed, is ever triumphant.

All this is founded on a fable because there is no God, and miracles are impossible. Christ is attacked in His Gospels as He was in life. "They sought false witness against Him, that they might put Him to death."[1] "Many bore false witness against Him, but their evidence was not agreeing."[2] All theories respecting the origin of the Gospels are shattered on the hard, impregnable rock of historic truth. The Evangelists narrate as they have the words and works of Jesus, only for one reason, because He so taught and acted. They may ask, as their Master before them, If I say the truth to you, why do you not believe Me?[3] And His accusers were silent.

---

[1] Matt. xxvi. 59. [2] Mark xiv. 56.
[3] John viii. 46.

CHAPTER V

THE DIVINITY OF CHRIST

FAITH in Christ being a condition of salvation, it was necessary that His Divinity should be attested by external proofs of a kind patent to all. These proofs are found, as has been said, in the marvellous and preternatural facts which marked His earthly life. We shall therefore now consider His miracles as evidence for His Divinity.

When the Baptist's disciples came by his desire to ask Christ whether He were the expected Messiah, Jesus, making answer, said: "Go and relate to John what you have heard and seen, the blind see, the lame walk, the lepers are cleansed, the deaf hear, the dead rise again, the poor have the Gospel preached to them." Thus He appeals to His miracles as the seal and witness to His mission, and He does so repeatedly throughout His public life. If at times He forbade the publication of the wonders wrought, this was only for special reasons, as, *e.g.*, for the spiritual benefit of the person healed. The character of His teaching demanded, indeed, some such display of preternatural power, for He taught, not by argument or proof, but on His own authority, "Amen,

Amen, I say to you:" and His works are the guarantee of His claim, and by them He stands or falls. His enemies understood His miracles in this sense, and ascribed them to the devil; but He insists on this proof of the Divinity they present. "If I by Beelzebub cast out devils, by whom do your children cast them out? But if I by the Spirit of God cast out devils, then is the kingdom of God come upon you."[1] They show His power to be divine, and one with His Father's. "For as the Father raiseth up the dead and giveth life, so the Son also giveth life to whom He will."[2] They are a stronger testimony, because more immediate and convincing, than the Baptist's, who produced no miraculous effects. "But I have a greater testimony than that of John; for the works which the Father hath given Me to perfect, the works themselves which I do, give testimony of Me; that the Father hath sent Me."[3] They prove Him the consubstantial Son of the Father. "The Father, who abideth in Me, He doeth the works."[4] Further, His works explain His words, and furnish their application. "Our Lord and Redeemer," says St. Gregory the Great, "speaks to us sometimes by His words, and at others by His deeds."[5] "What was hidden and mysterious in His teaching becomes apparent in His works."[6]

---

[1] Matt. xii. 28, 29.   [2] John v. 21.   [3] John v. 36.
[4] John xiv. 10.   [5] *Homil.* xxxii. *in Evang.*
[6] St. Aug., *Civ. Dei.*, xxii. 5, 8.

Himself the Light of the world in its darkness and ignorance, He gives bodily sight to the blind, He heals the sick of the palsy to prove His power to absolve from the paralysis of sin; as Nature's Creator and Lord, and the Great Comforter of souls, He calms the winds and waves; He multiplies the loaves, because He is Himself the Bread from Heaven which all must eat. As the Life of the world and its Redeemer, He raises the dead to life; and He cures all manner of infirmity, because He had come to make all things new, and as a pledge of Heaven to come.

What, then, is the evidence for the occurrence of Christ's miracles? The first miracle detailed fully by St. John[1] will show the scrutiny to which they were subjected. A beggar, blind from his birth, asked alms of our Lord by the wayside, and was told by Him to wash in the pool of Siloe. He went, and returned with his sight restored. The neighbours, seeing his miraculous cure, doubted, at least some of them, whether it could be the same man, and brought him to the Pharisees. His identity and the miracle being undoubtedly proved, some asked how such a sinner as our Lord could work so great a wonder. Others tried, but in vain, to intimidate the blind man's parents, who, however, confirmed the fact. Finally, unable to invent any further plea for rejecting this proof of our Lord's power, the Pharisees revile Him and cast Him out. Such is too often the

[1] John ix. 1.

"scientific" treatment of a miracle. First, the fact is denied, and then, when its truth proves incontestable, it is forcibly suppressed.

Next, consider the character of the evidence in support of the miracles. They are related by eye-witnesses,[1] or by those who, like St. Luke, derived their accounts from those who saw them.[2] These witnesses were themselves, as has been said, naturally incredulous, nor would they have their disciples believe on light or insufficient ground, or "give heed," as St. Paul says, "to fables;" but their faith is to be founded on the great fact of the Resurrection, confirmed as it was by the miracles of the Apostles, and the daily miraculous operations witnessed in the Church.[3]

Again, the miracles of Christ were wrought, not, as Renan says, in secret, but openly, and were public facts. Thus, St. Paul, in his appeal to Agrippa, says: "For the king knoweth of these things, to whom also I speak with confidence. For I am persuaded that none of these things are hidden from him. For neither were any of these things done in a corner.[4]

[1] 1 John i. 1, 2. [2] Luke i. 1 ff.
[3] St. Paul, in the following passages: Rom. xii. 4–8; Gal. iii. 5; 1 Cor. x. 28: appeals to miracles wrought by himself in the power of the Name of Jesus. He here testifies partly to his own works, partly to the miracles wrought in the Churches, which only confirm the works of the Lord, and even expressly refer to them. Besides the passages already quoted, see Heb. ii. 4: "God also bearing them witness by signs ($\sigma\eta\mu\epsilon\iota o\iota s$), and wonders ($\tau\epsilon\rho a\sigma\iota$), and divers miracles ($\pi o\iota\kappa\iota\lambda a\iota s$ $\delta\upsilon\nu\alpha\mu\epsilon\sigma\iota$), and distributions of the Holy Ghost according to His own Will."
[4] Acts xxvi. 26.

These wonders were effected in populous cities, amid crowds[1] of Greeks and Romans, sceptics and scoffers, and the Pagan inhabitants of the surrounding country,[2] before men of family, position, and culture.[3] They excited the envy of the popular leaders, and even attracted the attention of the king.[4]

Secondly, Christ's miracles were, for the most part, great manifestations of power, calculated to arrest the attention of multitudes. The multiplication of the loaves, the healing of the blind, the raising of the dead, were such as could be generally known and attested; and their first and most important result was the conversion of many, who proved the reality of their conviction by suffering and dying for the faith they had espoused.[5]

Again, they were wrought both in His presence, and at a distance,[6] by a single word, or by His simple unspoken Will;[7] mostly without preparation, or the use of outward means. And even when means are employed, such as the laying on of hands, anointing with spittle, or the like, they are used, not as instruments, but as symbols of the divine action in the orders of nature and grace, and bear no natural relation to the immediate, miraculous effects produced.

---

[1] Luke vi. 7 ; Matt. xi. 5 ; Mark i. 32 ; ii. 3.
[2] Luke vi. 17 ; Matt. viii. 9.
[3] Mark iii. 22 ; John iv. 46.
[4] John xi. 47 ; Luke xxiii. 8.
[5] John xi. 45 : "Many therefore of the Jews who came to Mary and Martha, and had seen the things that Jesus did, believed in Him."
[6] Matt. viii. 13 ; John iv. 52.   [7] John ix. 7 ; Mark v. 29.

His healing and vivifying word recalls the Creative Fiat; the clay and spittle the formation of Adam's body; His breathing on the Apostles the infusion into the lifeless mould of the breath of life. Thus, these same actions both recalled His omnipotent power exercised in the past, and foreshadowed His redemptive operation through the Church's future sacraments wherein similar means are employed.

Again, our Lord works His miracles with the majesty of One conscious of His sovereign power,[1] without anxiety or effort; and the greatest with the same calm dignity as the least. What is miraculous in man is natural in Him; such is the conviction of the crowds gathered round. The Roman centurion expresses the thought of all: "Only say the word, and my servant shall be healed."[2]

Still, it is objected, Christ wrought His cures by secret natural forces, known to Him alone. What, then, were the natural forces which could raise the dead to life, still the tempest, and restore sight to the blind, simply in obedience to a human will? Or how could the Son of a carpenter,[3] without education, surpass all men of His own and succeeding ages in His knowledge of nature and her resources? Or is it probable, if such power were His, that One "who went about doing good,"[4] whose whole life was love, should have wilfully hidden for ever a secret so much needed by suffering Humanity. His enemies strove by every means in their power to depreciate His

[1] Mark i. 22. [2] Matt. viii. 8. [3] John vii. 15. [4] Acts x. 38.

miracles, but never ascribed them to natural causes. It was reserved for the enlightened Rationalism of our day to represent, with Julian the Apostate of old, the Sage of Nazareth as an erudite physician.

Thus Renan attributes the raising of Lazarus partly to his recovery from a swoon, partly to intentional deception. The multiplication of the loaves he explains by the extraordinary care employed in their distribution; the exorcism of the possessed by the admiration felt by those unhappy persons for our Lord's personal beauty. Even Strauss condemns this treatment of the Gospel narrative, by which the discourses are retained and the actions rejected, as unphilosophical and unhistorical. Both form part of the same account, and a life of Christ without the miracles is like a life of Alexander or Cæsar from which their campaigns and victories have been eliminated.[1]

Hence, this explanation of miracles is abandoned by every later critic. Keim himself observes that "no sane person has ever supposed the Gospels to be based solely upon recent legends or modern inventions."[2] It is indisputable that they contain many actual historic facts, and it is equally indisputable that the words attributed by them to our Lord were uttered by Him; is it then conceivable that the great miracles by which they are accompanied should be pure inventions? Why are so many miracles recorded of Jesus, and none of the Baptist? Contrast also the

[1] Tholuck. [2] *Geschichte Jesu von Nazareth*, 1872, p. 140.

spontaneity of these miracles of healing with some of those of the Old Testament. Elias, like Eliseus later, raised the widow's son to life by measuring himself on the dead body three times, and crying upon God that the soul might return.¹ Our Lord performs the same wonder on the widow's son at Nain by His simple word: "Young man, I say to thee, arise."² Eliseus purified the spring of water by casting in salt from a new vessel.³ Our Lord turned the water at Cana to wine by His unspoken Will.⁴ Naaman is healed of his leprosy by the same prophet⁵ only after he had washed seven times in the Jordan. The ten lepers are made clean by our Lord⁶ immediately upon the utterance of His word.

Let us consider further the motive of Christ's miracles. Were they of a kind to conquer the spectator by the terrors of omnipotence, and to compel the incredulous to believe? The Pharisees ask of Him a sign from Heaven as a test of His miraculous power:⁷ our Lord is silent. When He is denied admission into a city of Samaria, and His disciples ask Him to call down fire from Heaven,⁸ our Lord gently exhorts them to patience. Herod⁹ and his court besiege Him with questions, hoping to see some miracle wrought by Him: one such miracle would have secured Him freedom and safety, and the favour of the court. Our Lord is silent, and

---

[1] 3 Kings xvii. 21.   [2] Luke vii. 14.   [3] 4 Kings ii. 20.
[4] John ii. 7–10.   [5] 4 Kings v. 10.   [6] Luke xvii. 14.
[7] Matt. xii. 38.   [8] Luke iv. 54.   [9] Luke xxiii. 8.

Herod treats Him as a fool. Yet, unasked, He heals the ear of His assailant, the High-priest's servant, and then suffers Himself to be taken captive and bound. A legendary account, an apocryphal Gospel, would have embellished the scene with miracles, and have put into Christ's mouth a well-set speech, such as that of Socrates. Divine Faith alone can discover Omnipotence under the bonds of a captive, or the Eternal Wisdom in a fool's robe. From His first public miracle at the marriage of Cana to His latest in Gethsemane, not one was wrought merely to gratify curiosity or to display His might, but to win the assent of those who were willing to believe. And the objects of His choice were ever the suffering and the afflicted. His healing power is evoked by Martha and Mary at their brother's grave, by the widowed mother at the bier of her son, by the blind beggar at the wayside, by the sick woman who touches in faith the hem of His garment. The one exception is the "cursing of the fig-tree,"[1] and even here the whole transaction is symbolical, a fulfilment of our Lord's words of the cutting down and burning of the tree without fruit, the type of faithless Israel.

But if our Lord's Divinity be seen in His miraculous works, it is no less manifested when His Almighty Power is restrained. It was by His humility, self-renunciation, annihilation of Himself and all that was His, by a moral miracle far surpassing His wonders in

---

[1] Matt. xxi. 19-23; Mark xi. 12-14, 20, 21. *Cf.* St. Augustine, En. in Ps. xxxi. 9.

HIS SELF-SACRIFICE A MORAL MIRACLE 139

the physical order, that Christ convinced His disciples of His unapproachable greatness. They saw Him hunger, who could turn stones into bread; they heard Him cry "I thirst," who was Himself the Living Water; they beheld Him die in torment, although He could have annihilated His enemies by a word. It was the contemplation of their Master's self-sacrifice which kindled the fire of love in their hearts, and urged them to suffer and to die for Him. In all his Epistles St. Paul sets forth our Lord's spontaneous self-oblation, His voluntary sufferings and death as the stamp and seal of His Divinity, and the very stigmata and the Cross of Christ are alone the Apostle's aureole.

To His voluntary death succeeded the miraculous Resurrection of Christ as the final proof of His Divinity and the fitting crown and completion of His work upon earth. "I have power," He says, "to lay down My life, and I have power to take it up again."[1] And He who uttered these words fulfilled them by His own Divine Will. The Resurrection is the triumph of our Lord over His enemies, the seal of His truth, the pledge of our salvation and future resurrection to glory. Death is the penalty of sin; had our Lord not risen again, the work of redemption would have failed, and our faith would, as St. Paul says, have been in vain. Without the Resurrection, Christianity falls. Instead of the God Man, the new Adam, in whom, according to the

[1] John x. 18.

divine plan, the history of man begins anew, there remains only the memory of One who died for His convictions, and the stream of history flows unbroken over His grave: By the preaching of the Resurrection, Christianity came into the world, and by faith in the Resurrection it triumphed. Further, Christ's victory over death and the grave impressed so strongly upon the minds of Christians the doctrine of the resurrection of the body, that we find it in advance of other dogmas in the second century, set forth and defended in formal theological treatises, notably by Athenagoras [1] and Tertullian.[2]

The Resurrection of our Lord presupposes the reality of His death. The fact is proved by the unanimous testimony of the Evangelists,[3] and by St. Paul;[4] by the fearful sufferings of the Crucifixion, which made death a physical certainty; by the violence and hatred of His enemies, who would only deliver up His body as a mutilated corpse, and after it had received the thrust of the confector's lance. It is further confirmed by the refusal of Pilate to deliver up the body till assured officially by the Centurion that Christ was really dead. Again, its reality is certified in the embalming of the Sacred Body by the Mother of the Lord and the holy women, who bound it in linen clothes with spices, "as is the custom of the Jews to bury," and who would have

---

[1] *De Resurrectione mortuorum.*   [2] *De Resurrectione carnis.*
[3] Matt. xxvii. 50; Mark xv. 37; Luke xxiii. 46; John xix. 30.
[4] 1 Cor. xv. 12.

been the first to discern any lingering spark of life. Finally, the reality of Christ's death has been admitted by the enemies of Christianity of all classes, down to the Jewish traditions of our own day.

But did Christ indeed rise again ? His Resurrection was the one sign which, under the image of the reappearance of Jonah from the whale's belly, He deigned to give the incredulous Pharisees. He made it the supreme proof of His divine nature and mission. " Destroy this temple," He says, " and in three days I will raise it up."[1] Nor did the Jews forget His words; they formed the ground of their accusations before the council and Pilate.[2]

So, too, when He had risen, He declared to His sorrowing disciples on the way to Emmaus that His victory over death was the crown of His work on earth. The fact of the Resurrection was publicly and repeatedly declared and attested ; first by the Magdalen who sought Him at dawn with the holy women, and to whom, as she wept, the Lord appeared.[3] The fact was declared by the Eleven, who, however, would not accept the women's testimony, and only believed after our Lord appeared to them Himself, ate and drank with them, and reproached them for their incredulity.[4] It is guaranteed, beyond the possibility of doubt, by the precautions taken by the Chief Priests and Pharisees, and by the Guard set at the tomb, who proclaimed

---

[1] John ii. 19. [2] Matt. xxvi. 61 ; xxvii. 39, 40.
[3] John xx. 18: "Mary Magdalen cometh and telleth the disciples, I have seen the Lord." [4] John xxi. 7, 12, 13.

through Jerusalem that Christ had risen, till they were bribed to say that during their sleep at night, Christ's Body had been stolen by His disciples. A statement which contradicts itself, for how could the soldiers have witnessed what occurred in their sleep? Yet it is the explanation adopted by Jewish controversialists down to the present time. "What sayest thou, then, O miserable cunning," writes St. Augustine. "Thou summonest sleeping witnesses. Truly thou sleepest thyself, that in searching such devices hast failed."[1]

Again, is it probable that the Apostles, who denied their Master, when dying, should have found courage to steal His Body, when dead? Or, if so, of what use would His Corpse have been to them, and how and where did they conceal it? As to this hypothesis —of wilful fraud on the part of the Apostles—Strauss says: "No lie of their own invention could possibly have inspired the disciples to proclaim the Resurrection of Christ with such steadfast courage amid the greatest danger; and Christian apologists rightly point to the amazing change from the utter despondency and hopelessness of the Apostles after the death of their Lord, to the enthusiastic faith with which, at Pentecost, they proclaimed Him to be the Messias. How account, they say, for this, unless meanwhile an extraordinary event had taken place, which inspired them with courage, and convinced them that the Crucified Jesus was indeed risen again?"[2]

[1] In Ps. lxiii., Oxford trans.   [2] *Leben Jesu*, 3rd ed., ii. p. 685.

The theory, then, of the simulated death of Christ, and of the abstraction of His Body, being proved untenable, and the reality of the disciples' faith in the Resurrection being attested beyond doubt by their sufferings and death endured in witness thereof, one other attempt has been made by Strauss, Renan, and others, to account for the Resurrection on natural grounds, viz., that the witnesses were themselves deceived by imaginary visions. M. Renan says: "Henoch and Elias had not tasted death. People began even to believe that the patriarchs and other eminent men of the Old Testament had not really died, but that their bodies were still living in their graves at Hebron! As with other men who have gained the veneration of their contemporaries, so with Jesus; the world, accustomed to ascribe to such men supernatural powers, refuses to believe that they could be subjected to the unjust law of death. Heroes never die. Their beloved Master had so lived in and with those around Him, that after His death, they could not but maintain that He would live for ever. On the day after His entombment, this feeling was uppermost in their minds; the women, above all, rendered Him service with tender devotion. 'Surely,' said they, 'angels surround Him and veil their faces in His shroud.' On that day the little company of Christians brought to pass the true miracle; by the mighty love they bore Him, they brought Jesus to life again in their hearts. They determined that Jesus should not die. In such decisive moments a gust of wind, a creaking window, a sudden murmuring sound, decides for ages the faith of nations. On that day for an hour, Mary of Magdala upheld the whole fabric of Christian consciousness."[1]

But Strauss's own objection to the theory of deception on the part of the disciples applies equally to this hypothesis of a vision. Why and how, dismayed and discouraged as they were, should the Apostles have suddenly become so convinced of the truth of the Resurrection as to create a phantom and proclaim it as real? The idea of an anticipated resurrection, that is, of the bodies of the dead being raised before the Judgment Day, was unknown in our Lord's time, and no trace of it appears in the Old Testament. The belief in the miraculously prolonged life of Henoch and Elias formed no basis for supposing that one, visibly dead, could live again, but, on the contrary, would prove a strong objection to such an hypothesis. Again, why did not the Sanhedrim produce the dead Christ? Even Baur owned, at the close of his life, that "an impenetrable mystery hangs over the time between the Death and Resurrection of Christ, and that by a chain of facts, first violently broken, then miraculously renewed, we find ourselves on a totally new platform of the history."[2] But in St. Paul we have the undisputed evidence of one to whom the myth theory is wholly inapplicable, for up to the moment of his conversion he had been a fanatical

---

[1] *Les Apôtres*, chap. i.
[2] Cf. *Engelhardt, Schenkel, and Strauss*, 1864, p. 85.

ST. PAUL'S INDEPENDENT EVIDENCE 145

persecutor of the followers of the Christian name. Yet, twenty years after the death of Christ, and before the Gospels were written, St. Paul proclaims the Death, Burial, and Resurrection of Christ as the groundwork of the faith, and explicitly declares that He (Christ) was seen by Cephas, by the Eleven, by more than five hundred brethren at once, "of whom many remain to this present, and some are fallen asleep;" again "by James, then by all the Apostles, and last of all by me as one born out of due time."[1] Here then he speaks of an objective, external bodily form as distinctly witnessed by himself and others, and in very different language from that which he uses to describe a vision; as, for instance, when lifted up "to the third Heaven, whether in the body or out of the body I know not," or (by the hand of St. Luke) when "the man of Macedonia comes to him by night;" or again, how precisely he distinguishes the effect on his senses in the moment of his actual conversion, "hearing a voice, but seeing no one." What, then, was the cause of his conversion? Renan feels the difficulty, and attributes the vision of the Risen Christ to inflammation of the eyes, caught by St. Paul in the sudden transition from the scorching steppes of the Damascus road to the shady gardens of the city itself! Assuredly, the transformation of Saul, the fanatical persecutor, into Paul the Apostle is an overwhelming testimony to the power of Christ, a fact which alone suffices to

[1] 1 Cor. xv. 3-8.

K

refute all objections against the divine origin of Christianity.

Finally, if all the reported occurrences of the forty days after Easter are mythical, whence came the grand, majestic utterances of the Risen Christ, predicting the development of His Kingdom? For it is incredible that these visionary, hysterical, timorous disciples,—as M. Renan depicts them,—themselves invented words so opposed to all their Jewish prejudices, as the command to baptize, the power of absolution, and the promise of the Church's enduring stability throughout all ages.

"But why," asks Celsus, "did not Christ, by showing Himself openly to His enemies, constrain them to believe in Him?"[1] Because, as we have seen,[2] the fact of the Resurrection, though effected in secret, was sufficiently proved; the miracles wrought by the Apostles corroborated the truth of their own witness to the fact. Those who rejected the Apostles' miracles would equally have denied the truth and identity of the Risen Jesus. Moreover, like all other miracles, that of the Resurrection has a deep moral significance, and was not worked to satisfy the curiosity of wilful unbelievers. Finally, His atoning Death closed our Lord's mission upon earth; Israel had had

---

[1] Origen, *C. Celsus*, ii. 63.
[2] Acts iv. 14, 16, 18: "They could say nothing against it." . . . "For indeed a known miracle hath been done by them, before all the inhabitants of Jerusalem; it is manifest, and we cannot deny it." . . . "And calling them, they charged them not to speak at all, nor teach in the Name of Jesus."

its trial and was now condemned. Israelites still came as believers to the feet of the Apostles; but Israel, as a nation, had pronounced its own judgment; and the words, "You shall seek Me, and shall not find Me," were now fulfilled. Thus, after His Resurrection, our Lord no longer preached to the Jews; He only manifested Himself to His disciples, "speaking to them of the Kingdom of God,"[1] for to them the office of preaching was now transferred.

The hypotheses of modern sceptics are only a repetition of those objections which Celsus puts into the mouth of an unbelieving Jew. He is made to ask, "Who saw it? A fanatical woman—the 'femme hallucinée' of Renan—practised in such jugglery, who was either deceived by her diseased and morbid fancies, and mistook a phantom for a reality, as many have done; or else (which seems to me more probable) was herself the author of this deception, in order to astonish others or delude them into the same lie."[2] But thousands of all classes, besides our Lord's disciples, attested the fact of the Resurrection, in spite of the threats of the Synagogue and the report of the Body being stolen, and upon faith in this miracle the Church is founded, and its foundation constitutes the turning point in the world's history which can be explained in no other way. And if we would be convinced of the impossibility of devising any intelligible substitute for the Gospel of history, we have only to read the latest attempts of Renan,

[1] Acts i. 3.   [2] Origen, *C. Celsus*, ii. 45.

Schenkel, and Strauss to represent Jesus of Nazareth as a merely human moral teacher. Neither mythical theories, imaginary Resurrections, nor forged Gospels offer escape from the one alternative. Christ is either the Incarnate Son of God, as described in the Gospels, or a proved impostor. If He were the latter, and His Resurrection was not a real fact, then in Dante's words—

> "That all the world, said I, should have been turned
> To Christian, and no miracle been wrought,
> Would in itself be such a miracle
> The rest were not an hundredth part so great." [1]

Two of the Church's greatest doctors had, before Dante, already expressed this thought. "It would indeed," says St. Thomas, "have been the most amazing of miracles if, without any miraculous signs, a few simple, unknown men had persuaded the world to embrace a faith so far beyond man's comprehension, which entailed obligations so onerous, and anticipated a future so sublime." [2] "The Resurrection alone," says St. Augustine,[3] "could ever have inspired the disciples with faith in the Church, and in the future of Christianity; but we who have the Church before us, are certain that Christ rose from the dead. But if any one believes that the Apostles wrought no miracles when they preached the Resurrection and Ascension of Christ, this miracle alone would suffice us; namely, that the whole world believed without miracle."

[1] *Parad.* xxiv. 108.   [2] *Cont. Gent.*, i. 6.   [3] *Civ. Dei.*, xxii. 5.

CHAPTER VI

PROPHECY AND FULFILMENT

FIRST a pastoral, then an agricultural people, Israel presents in her history no record of great undertakings, of political power, of military conquests like those of Assyria, Babylon, or Rome. Nor have her sons left their mark in the realm of thought, as founders of philosophical schools, or again, in the domain of art, painting, sculpture, architecture, that marvellous sense of beauty and form, in all of which the Greeks excelled. For the most part, the current of her life flows on, calm and uneventful, free from the tumult of popular movements, every man dwelling under "his own vine and his own fig-tree."[1] Yet, as the chosen people of God, and the guardian of His revelation, the influence of Israel has been of supreme importance; and her Sacred Books, in the sublimity of their doctrine, the purity of their moral teaching, and the simplicity and sobriety of their style, attest a more than human origin.

Without the sensuous splendour, the fantastic speculations of the Hindoo writings, Hebrew literature finds in the One Personal God of Revelation its sublime

[1] 3 Kings iv. 25.

ideal and its fixed limits. As in later times, Hellenic genius reduced the gigantic and often grotesque representations of Eastern art to the proportions of human beauty, so amidst the fantastic chaos of Eastern mythology, the religion of Israel stands forth in calm, unobtrusive dignity, as the organ of divine truth. And this contrast is more marked as we extend our view. Pantheism had impregnated the ancient world. Nature and its forces were the one object of worship, and its good or evil genius, as displayed in the annual cycle of growth or decay, was to be propitiated by a corresponding cultus of sensuality, or of mortification which were alike unrestrained. Not so with the Hebrews. The earth was indeed the Lord's and the fulness thereof; but not to the operations of nature did Israel look for a clue to the Providence of God; but to His dealings with man, and above all, with the people of His choice.

Of more importance than their outward prosperity was their inward life, and whether they were accounted just or sinners in His sight. They knew they were not mere blind material atoms, produced only to be reabsorbed in the ever recurring cycle of nature, but free responsible agents, determining for themselves by their own moral life the progressive development of their history. Thus, while other nations round them worshipped the visible universe and its forces, Israel looked beyond the world to God. "The Greeks," says Heine, "were but beautiful youths; the Hebrews were always strong and steadfast men."

According to Renan,[1] Monotheism was the natural tendency of the Israelites, and of all Semitic nations —a statement, the value of which Max Müller thus appreciates: "To most people it may sound more philosophical to speak of a monotheistic instinct than of the true revelation of a living God. But is this instinct less mysterious than revelation? How can there be instinct unless it is the result of a definite inspiration? And whose hand implanted in the Semitic mind the faith in one God? Would the same Hand have implanted in the Arian mind the belief in a plurality of gods? Could the monotheistic instinct of the Semitic race, if it was really an instinct, have been so constantly obscured by the polytheistic instinct of the Arian race, or the polytheistic instinct of the Arian race have been so utterly destroyed that the Jews could come to worship strange gods on the heights of Jerusalem, and the Greeks and Romans become zealous Christians. Fishes never fly, nor do ants ever catch frogs. Such are the problems in which we are involved when we use words rather according to their sound than with regard to their sense."[2]

According to Strauss, the One God of Israel was nothing more than the idealised impersonation of her national self-consciousness, and was only relatively superior to the surrounding gods of Canaan which, from time to time, were also objects of their worship.

[1] *Journal Asiatique*, 1859; *Etudes d'histoire religieuse*, p. 85 ff.
[2] *Essays*, i. p. 293 ff.

As the Jewish people developed still further their higher instincts, Jehovah became a stern lawgiver, the avenger of sensuality and cruelty, and the worship of Him a school for chastity and morality.[1]

But facts refute this theory. The life of Israel as a nation begins with Revelation, messages from God, and miracles wrought on her behalf. Yet, though thus the special object of divine favour, the Jewish people appear in their history as constantly relapsing, by their natural corruption, into idolatry, and only brought back by the reproaches and threats of the prophets to the worship of the one true God. The revealed word and no natural tendency imparted to Israel a pure conception of the Deity, and an idea of creation, nowhere else fully realised. In keeping with the superiority of her creed is that of her morality; her code of laws defines and embraces all the duties of man in public or private, of ruler and subject, master and servant, rich and poor, husband and wife, with a precision, delicacy, and gentleness peculiar to itself. If certain passages in the Old Testament, for instance, those on polygamy, seem opposed to the tenor of a revealed code, we must remember that God, as man's preceptor, "leading him to Christ," tolerated much "because of the hardness of their hearts," and that the Decalogue is, and always will be, the foundation of our whole modern system of culture and morals. The Mosaic law stands midway between the two systems of divine education,

[1] *Die a'te und neue Glaube*, 6th ed., p. 1041.

THE GUARDIAN OF REVELATION 153

the Patriarchal and the Christian, and is in harmony with both. It contains elements capable of raising individuals to a high moral standard, although the restrictions which it imposed, and the veils under which the spiritual essence was concealed, hindered man and society from attaining the perfect fulfilment of their destiny.[1]

Thus Israel appears set apart as the destined guardian of the true religion ; her law awakening the consciousness of sin, and with its ritual and sacrifices renewing the expectation of the Redeemer. " All nations of antiquity in east or west," says Renan, " looked back to a golden age, for ever lost, and to Paradise as existing only at the beginning of all things.[2] Israel alone aspired to glories yet to come, and the more ardently as the present grew darker. In her maternal womb the salvation of the world was to be begotten ; silently and invisibly, but with sure and fixed progress ; and she forms herself, in her life and office, the type of the Virgin Mother who conceives, not of man but of God, and brings forth the Messias.[3]

Thus, too, notwithstanding its religious and political isolation, Israel held to the belief that one day its

[1] *Cf.* Haneberg, *ibid.*, p. 146.
[2] *Vie de Jesus*, 2nd ed., p. 11. "In Cicero's writings we vainly seek for a single expression of hope as regards the progressive amelioration of mankind. The two poles of his philosophy between which he incessantly oscillates are lamentation over the past and resignation as regards the present " (Merivale, *History of the Romans,* ii 538).
[3] " For salvation is of the Jews " (John iv. 22).

religion would be that of the whole world; and since this religion was not the product of the national spirit nor "a wild olive tree,"[1] a merely natural growth, it did not, like the heathen religions, perish with the race from which it sprung. As a nation, Israel fell, but Israel's religion, cast off by the majority of its people and transplanted from its birthplace, lived on, and commenced a career of universal conquest, as the Church of Christ.

This intimate connection, wonderful in design and accomplishment, between the Old and New Covenants, the law and the prophets, between Moses and Christ, subsisting as it did throughout centuries, proves the divine origin of both dispensations; since only a Mind to whom "a thousand years are but as a day" could order and carry out this great harmonious scheme. "If," says Pascal, "a single man had written a book of prophecies of Jesus Christ; if Christ had actually appeared at the time and in the manner foretold, this would be a proof of the working of an Infinite spiritual power; but here there is far more. We find a succession of men who, during four thousand years, continually, and without variation, foretold this same event."[2]

Let us consider the evidence from prophecy under the three following heads: The universal expectation of a Messias among Jews and Gentiles; its prediction by the Prophets; its fulfilment in Jesus Christ.

The expectation of Messias meets us in every page

[1] Rom. xi. 17.　　[2] *Pensées*, Part II. art. 11.

of the Gospels. "Art thou He that art to come," ask the disciples of St. John Baptist, "or look we for another?" Priests and Levites had already questioned Him by their messengers: "Who art thou?"[1] For all were doubting in their hearts whether he were not the promised Messias.[2] "But he confessed and did not deny; and confessed, I am not the Christ."[3] Even the woman of Samaria speaks of Christ's approaching Advent as of an event expected by all men.[4]

And this was no undefined, vague conception, no mere ideal of a glorious future, the dream of enthusiastic patriots; for the conditions under which He was to appear, His genealogy, the time and place of His birth, His titles, offices, and work were, in all essential points, known to the Jews who were contemporaries of Jesus Christ.[5]

Thus, when Herod asked the Scribes and Priests where the Messias should be born, they at once replied, according to the prophecy: Bethlehem in the land of Judah, as prophesied by Micheas;[6] He is of

[1] John i. 19. [2] Luke iii. 15. [3] John i. 20. [4] John iv. 25.
[5] According to Strauss (*Glaubenslehre*, i. p. 222), there are no Messianic prophecies, " but simply a presentiment among the leading minds of the Jewish nation that there would be in the future a great development of the religion of Jehovah." Yet, only a few years before, Strauss made the Messianic prophecies, as applied by the Evangelists to their Master, the basis of the mythical Christ. In his *Leben Jesu* (vol. i. § 12, p. 73), he says: "In Him all the Messianic prophecies of the Old Testament were to find their fulfilment; otherwise he could not have corresponded to the Messianic idea, already delineated by the Jews."
[6] Matt. ii. 6.

the line of David, and cannot therefore come out of Galilee;[1] He is to be a King over Israel;[2] the great Prophet[3] and Priest;[4] the Son of God, armed with divine power and manifesting the divine Life;[5] He will inaugurate a dispensation of Salvation, in which all things will appear in a new divine order; through Him His people will be absolved from their sins;[6] He will reign over His people in everlasting beatitude,[7] which shall flow forth from out of Israel into all nations.[8]

This expectation of the immediate Advent of the Messias is vividly expressed in Zachary's canticle of praise.[9] Looking back on the long line of prophets, extending in an unbroken series throughout Israel's history, he now sees their predictions fulfilled; for with the birth of the Precursor the work of Redemption has begun, and the Advent of Messias is at hand. Again, the aged Simeon declares that his eyes have seen the Lord's Salvation, the Light of the Gentiles, and the Glory of His people Israel.[10] Finally, St. John Baptist himself points to Him, now manifested, Who, though coming after him, yet was before him; and gives testimony that He is the Son of God.[11]

Non-inspired writings furnish also proofs of the expectation of the Messias in the national mind. The Chaldee paraphrases of the Pentateuch by Onkelos,

---

[1] John viii. 41-43.
[2] Matt. ii. 2; xxi. 5; Luke xxiii. 2, 3; John vi. 15.
[3] John vi. 14. [4] Luke i. 77. [5] John xi. 27; xii. 34.
[6] Matt. iii. 2, 11. [7] John xvii. 34. [8] Luke i. 77-79.
[9] Luke i. 68 ff. [10] Luke ii. 30-32. [11] John i. 34.

and those of the prophets by Jonathan Ben Usiel, constantly express the idea of His coming, and these writings were extant, if not before, at any rate in the time of Christ, and were of high reputation among the Jews. From these sources Josephus wrote the history of his nation. He describes the false Messias, each in turn declaring himself to be the expected one, and ascribes the secret of their ephemeral success to the world-wide belief of the people in the Ruler, predicted by Daniel[1] and the other prophets, Who was to arise from their midst.[2] It was the false expectation of the Messias as a temporal ruler which led to Israel's ruin. Worldliness and ambition induced them to reject the Christ and to prefer impostors, who, by their promises of political aggrandisement and temporal dominion, incited them to repeated revolts. Hence followed the vengeance of Rome, the destruction of the Temple, and the dispersion of the race. The advent of Christ and His world-wide kingdom, with its conflicts and victories; Sion and the Mount of the Temple; the confluence of all nations to the Holy City; its abounding prosperity; all the glorious symbolism of the prophets, were not to be interpreted in a temporal or literal manner, but of the Church to come. The establishment of the kingdom of God in the plenitude of eternal glory is to be realised only

[1] *Antiq.*, x. 11.
[2] It is true that, in order to flatter Vespasian, Josephus himself applied these prophecies to that emperor, but he acknowledges that this is contrary to the tradition of his people (*Bell. Jud.*, vi. 5).

with the second advent of the Messias at the final term of all things.

But the traces of the Messianic idea appear, notwithstanding the hopelessness of their future, even among heathen nations at that time. Tacitus tells us that, " according to the predictions of the ancient sacred writings the East would become powerful, and that men from Judæa would found an universal empire."[1] "Throughout the East," says Suetonius, "there was an ancient, unchanging tradition that men out of Judæa would found a new and universal empire."[2] Cicero observes that the ancient prophecies foretold the coming of a King to Whom men must do homage in order that they may be saved; and he asks himself who would this be, and when He should come?[3] And Virgil describes this new era, foretold by the Sybil, in which a mysterious Babe should be born, Son of the Godhead, by Whom all creation would be renewed, the serpent destroyed, sin blotted out, and peace restored to the earth.[4]

And this expectation could only have arisen from primal tradition not wholly lost, or from the reiterated prophecies of Israel. Inscribed on the first pages of her sacred books was the promise of the Saviour, born of a woman, who was to bruise the serpent's head;[5] and this promise is three times repeated: He is to be born of a woman; a descendant of Abraham in Whom and in Whose seed all the earth is to be blest.[6] The

---

[1] *Annals*, v. 13. [2] *In vita Vespas.*, c. 4. [3] *De divin.*, ii. 54.
[4] *Eclog.* iv. [5] Gen. iii. 15. [6] Gen. xii. 3; xviii. 18; xxii. 18.

promise is renewed to Isaac, and again to Jacob,¹ who transmits it on his death-bed to Juda, with the prophecy that the tribe of Judah would be the ruler of the twelve, and that the advent of the Shilo (the peace or the rest) would coincide with the loss of Judah's sovereignty.²

Thus, from the Patriarchal age there was a definite forecast of Him Who was to come. Still more distinctly was He announced in the Mosaic period. Balaam prophesied His victory over the enemies of Israel.³ Moses, with his last breath, proclaims the great Prophet, like himself a Mediator, Founder of a New Covenant, a Lawgiver whom God will raise up.⁴ When a king is given to Israel in the person of David, he is the prototype of the King Who is to come; the Messias, that is, the Anointed One; the special protector of the lowly, the suffering, and the afflicted; the Ruler of the kingdom committed to Him by God; the offspring of David,⁵ Prophet, King,⁶ and High Priest, and of a sacerdotal order, not transient like that of Aaron, but like Melchisedech, lasting for ever. Christ is the absolute representative of God upon earth,⁷ and in His world-wide kingdom all the nations will find health and beatitude.⁸

In apparent contradiction to these images of power and glory is the Psalmist's portraiture of the sufferings of the Messias, so vividly delineated as to read rather

---

[1] Gen. xxvi. 4; xxviii. 14.   [2] Gen. xlix. 10.   [3] Num. xxiv. 17.
[4] Deut. xviii. 15-18.   [5] 2 Kings vii. 12.   [6] Ps. ii. 1.
[7] Ps. cix. 1.   [8] Ps. lxxi. 4, 5.

like narrative than prophecy.[1] The pain, scorn, and infamy to be endured by the "Just One" will exceed all that man has ever borne. He is the butt of His enemies, the outcast of the people, His accusers rejoice and mock at His sufferings, and for His vesture they cast lots. By His voluntary acceptance of these terrible and unmerited sufferings, He, the All-Holy, is at once Priest and Victim, the Mediator and Atonement for the sins of men, and the source of their salvation; for by His Passion and His Death the heathen shall be converted, and all nations shall adore the one true God.[2]

The prophets who come after the Assyrian and Babylonian captivity (B.C. 722–536), impress these ideas with ever increasing detail upon the consciousness of Israel. Micheas predicts that the Messias is to be born at Bethlehem.[3] Isaias declares that He shall be born in a supernatural manner of a Virgin.[4] He is the manifestation of God in the flesh and the Saviour of the Gentiles;[5] to Him are ascribed all the divine attributes; He is at once Prophet, Priest, and Victim; finally, King,[6] Redeemer, and Lord of all, as described in the Psalm.[7] At the same time, the sufferings of the Messias and His patience under them are minutely described.[8]

Daniel consoles the Hebrews of the Babylonian captivity by showing them the succession of the four

---

[1] Ps. xxi. 3 ff. [2] Ps. xxi. 23. [3] Micheas v. 2.
[4] Isa. vii. 14. [5] Isa. ix. 6.   [6] Isa. ix. 7.
[7] Ps. xxi. 27.   [8] Isa. liii. 1, 2.

great empires—the Assyrio-Babylonian, the Persian, the Grecian, and the Roman; and by pointing finally to the universal, never-ending Empire, which is to overwhelm and destroy all the others.[1]

At the same time Daniel indicates the epoch of the Messianic Kingdom. Following upon the seventy years of the Babylonian captivity, foretold by Jeremias, he announces the beginning of the full Redemption and true salvation of Israel at the end of seventy weeks of years, dating from the command for the rebuilding of Jerusalem.[2] Then their transgression will cease, all sin and guilt be pardoned, eternal justice manifested, the vision will be fulfilled, and the Saint of saints anointed. At the end of sixty-nine weeks, in the middle of the last week, the Covenant will be confirmed with many, the old sacrifices will come to an end, the Anointed will be slain, and the City and Sanctuary laid waste by the Gentiles.

However much critics may dispute the precise dates variously assigned for the beginning, or the term of the weeks of Daniel, "a world-wide, indisputable event has," says Bossuet, "lifted it above all the subtleties of chronologists. The total ruin of the Jewish nation, so soon after the death of Christ, must convince any fair-minded man that the prophecy has been fulfilled."[3] Definite periods of time are predicted elsewhere in Holy Scripture, as the sojourn of the Israelites in Egypt for four hundred years;[4] the

---

[1] Dan. ii. 44, 45.
[2] Dan. ix. 24–27.
[3] *Hist. Univ.*, p. 11.
[4] Gen. xv. 13.

restored prosperity of Tyre after seventy years of misery;[1] the destruction of Ephraim as a nation at the end of sixty-five years;[2] the prolongation of the life of Ezechias for fifteen years;[3] the seventy years of the Babylonian captivity.[4] Our Lord Himself applies the weeks of Daniel to the destruction of Jerusalem.[5]

Of the minor prophets, Aggeas foretold the erection of the second Temple,[6] made even more glorious than the first by the entry therein of the desired of the nations, the mighty God Himself.[7] Yet, says Zacharias, not in majesty and power will He come, but poor and lowly, riding on a colt, the foal of an ass.[8] Finally, Malachi, the last of the Prophets, sees the angel, the precursor of the Messias, approaching as a preacher of penance before the day of visitation. Then the Messias will appear. He will visit His Temple, and substitute for the rejected sons of Aaron a new priesthood, which will offer to God a pure sacrifice from the rising to the setting of the sun.[9]

The portrait of the Messias, thus growing in distinctness, sustained the hope of Israel, and interpreted in each generation the signs of the times; and though prophecy is essentially dim and mysterious, still, enough was given to enable the pure of heart—Israelites, like Nathanael, without guile—to recognise the Messias when He came.

---

[1] Isa. xxiii. 15-17. [2] Isa. vii. 8. [3] Isa. xxxviii. 5.
[4] Jer. xxv. 11. [5] Matt. xxiv. 15. [6] Of Zerubabel.
[7] Agg. ii. 7-9. [8] ix. 9-11. [9] Mal. iii. 1-4, 5, 10, 11; iii. 3.

Now, Jesus of Nazareth alone fulfils this long train of prophecies. He is a son of Abraham, of the tribe of Judah, of the family of David, born at Bethlehem, and of a Virgin. He is poor and lowly, but works miracles; dies in shame yet rises in glory, and He declares Himself the Christ foretold.[1] "I know," says the woman of Samaria, "that Messias cometh."[2] And Jesus answered her, "I am He." "Behold," He says, "we go up to Jerusalem, and all things shall be accomplished which were written in the prophets concerning the Son of Man."[3] "And beginning at Moses and all the prophets, He expounded to them in all the Scriptures the things that were concerning Him."[4] He claimed the dignity of King of the Jews;[5] for this He was tried and condemned; His regal title was nailed to His Cross.[6]

The Jewish people themselves supplied the proofs needed of His lineage and His mission; for He came at a time when each tribe preserved its genealogy, could trace its family register up to Abraham, and the political and religious order of the nation still existed. The legal sacrifices were yet offered by the priests of Aaron, and the Temple stood as the centre of the national covenant, the bond of union and the essential condition of worship.

But soon after the death of Christ, all this had

---

[1] Jesus (Saviour, Helper), indicates His office ; Messias (anointed), χριστος, His dignity. He is *the* Anointed, the one filled with the Spirit of God.   [2] John iv. 25.
[3] Luke xviii. 3.   [4] Luke xxiv. 27.
[5] John xix. 12 ; Acts xvii. 17.   [6] Matt. xxvii. 37.

vanished; and not by temporary bondage, as in the first captivity, but by final destruction. Israel is dispersed, the City and Temple are in ruins, the people without sacrifice and without altar, without Ephod and without Teraphim.[1] A new covenant, a new sacrifice and priesthood are established,[2] and the expectation of the Messias became thus an idle dream, or an accomplished fact.

The cause of Israel's apostasy has already been told; their desire of a temporal ruler, and their national exclusiveness, so opposed to the promised admission of the Gentiles to the New Covenant. Into that Covenant all that was best in Israel, the true children of Abraham, were already incorporated—Elizabeth, the Baptist, Anna, Zacharias, Simeon, Nathanael, Nicodemus, the thousands who believed in Him, the Apostles, St. Joseph, and, above all, the Mother of the Lord.[3] False Israel remained, as the prophets and the Scriptures described it, a stiffnecked and uncircumcised race, resisting, as their fathers had, the Holy Ghost;[4] and their carnal sense and ambitious desires were stimulated and encouraged by the Pharisees and their allies the Priests. The priesthood was degraded and venal; the Pharisees, proud of their legal knowledge, of their scrupulous observance of the law, filled with self-righteousness, regarded themselves as the elect of God. To such men nothing could be more galling than the influence of an un-

---

[1] *Osee.*, iii. 4. [2] Mal. i. 10, 11; Matt. xxvi. 26; 1 Cor. xi. 24.
[3] John i. 47. [4] Acts vii. 51.

CHRIST HIMSELF A PROPHET 165

lettered Galilean, who preached, as Christ did, an outward holiness, and condemned in strongest terms their merely external virtue—One who, while wholly indifferent to the disputes and the learning of their schools, could expose their ignorance and hypocrisy,[1] and by His knowledge of men's hearts reply to their unspoken thoughts. Here then were reasons more than sufficient for procuring His death.[2]

We have considered the evidence from the prophecies, so far as they are fulfilled in Christ. But our Lord is Himself the Founder of the New Covenant, a Prophet greater than Moses. As the Seers of the Old Law disclosed the future to Israel, and thus awakened her faith, so also our Lord traced out for His disciples the plan of the new Temple, whose foundations He had laid. And His prophetic word streams like a ray of light upon the remote future, enabling the believer to discern clearly the great events or crises as they are developed in the history of His Church.

Jesus Christ predicts those events about to happen to Himself[3] and to His Apostles;[4] He foretells His denial by Peter,[5] His betrayal by Judas[6] at a time when Peter refused to believe the one, and none of the disciples suspected the other.[7] He predicts the fate of His people, the destruction of the City and Temple,[8] with its circumstances—that it is to take

---
[1] Matt. xxi. 16, 23. [2] John xi. 47.
[3] Matt. xvii. 21; xx. 18; Mark x. 33; Luke ix. 44; John x. 17.
[4] Matt. x. 17; Luke xxi. 12. [5] Matt. xxvi. 33.
[6] John xiii. 21. [7] John xiii. 28, 29.
[8] Matt. xxiv. 2, 25; Mark xiii. 2; Luke xix. 42-44; xxi. 6.

place in "this" generation;¹ false prophets will arise;² one stone shall not remain upon another;³ finally He foretells the lasting dispersion of Israel among the nations.⁴

And all these events, when predicted by our Lord, were, humanly speaking, most improbable, and opposed to all political calculations. Yet history confirms their truth. Josephus relates that the people blindly followed every demagogue who claimed to be either a prophet, or the Precursor, or the Messias Himself. From Pheudas (A.D. 45) onwards, each decade produced its pseudo-prophets and pseudo-Messias.⁵ When the Temple was in flames six thousand men followed one of the false prophets, who promised to save them, into a covered way near the Temple, where they all perished. The contemporaries of our Lord survived the fate of the City and of the Temple, for the insurrection broke out in A.D. 66.⁶ The conflict lasted seven years, the Romans under Titus contesting each foot of ground. The intense hatred between Jews and Romans, the two proudest nations of the world, was shown in the merciless vengeance of the besiegers and the obstinate resistance of the besieged. Josephus roughly estimates the number of those who perished at a million.⁷ About ninety thousand were sold as slaves;⁸ starvation and sickness carried off even more than the sword.⁹ In opposition to the usual policy

---

¹ Matt. xxiv. 34.   ² Matt. xxiv. 5, 24.
³ Luke xxi. 6.   ⁴ Luke xxi. 24.
⁵ Josephus, *Bell. Jud.*, ii. 13; vi. 5; *Antiq.*, xx. 7.   ⁶ *Antiq.*, xx. 7.
⁷ *Bell. Jud.*, vi. 9.   ⁸ Luke xxi. 24.   ⁹ Luke xxi. 23.

of the Romans which spared the chief towns, and especially the sanctuaries, and in spite of the orders of Titus, both City and Temple were utterly destroyed. Many Jews living without the walls, who had come for the Paschal solemnities, were involved in the general ruin. The Christians alone, remembering the prophecy,[1] had left the city and taken refuge in Pella, a Greek colony on the other side of Jordan. This terrible fulfilment of their Master's prophecy must have served mightily to strengthen the faith of the infant Church in its struggle against the Synagogue, and its effects extended to many of the Jews; and the attempt of the Jews, with the help of the Emperor Julian, to falsify the prophecy by rebuilding the Temple and restoring the Mosaic worship, could not alter the fact of its fulfilment. The issue of that attempt is thus described. "As the Jews were diligently carrying on the building, Cyril, the Bishop of Jerusalem, said, 'In a short time there will not remain one stone upon another;' and so it was. By night, a mighty earthquake tore up the massive stones of the foundations of the Temple, and, with them, overthrew the adjacent buildings . . . fire from heaven consumed all the scaffoldings and all the workmen's materials, and continued to rage throughout the whole day."[2] Even could these awful phenomena be explained by natural causes, such as an earthquake or peculiar asphaltic conditions of the ground, still this

---

[1] Euseb., H. E., iii. 5 ; Epiph., *De pond. et mens.*, c. 5 ; Luke xxi. 5.
[2] Socrat., H. E., iii. 20.

does not take away the providential character of its occurrence, both as regards time and conditions, in conformity with the fact predicted. The dispersion of the Jews among all nations is indeed an isolated and unparalleled fact. As a rule, the stronger nationality absorbs the vanquished race. But Israel remains an alien among the nations, an attendant shadow wherever the Cross is upraised, a silent, yet eloquent witness to the Gospel's truth, and to her own reprobation.[1] "Those," says Pascal,[2] quoting St. Augustine,[3] "who rejected and crucified Christ, are the same who preserve the sacred books which witness against themselves, proclaiming and prophesying that He should be rejected and be a stumbling-block to them. God chose this nation, endowed with such singular zeal and endurance, in order that it might carry throughout the whole world those books which contain the prophecies of Christ, and display them openly before the eyes of all people."

Finally, Jesus predicted the world-wide spread of His Gospel, and the universal sway of His Church.[4] St. Paul was able to say that the Gospel had penetrated as far as Illyrium, and that the faith of the Romans was spoken of in the whole world.[5] According to Pliny, at the end of the first century Christianity had already overspread the whole empire, so that the festivals of the gods were no longer celebrated, and

---

[1] Rom. xi. 25, 26.
[2] *Pensées*, art. 8.
[3] *De Fide*, c. vi. n. 9.
[4] Acts i. 8; John xii. 32; Matt. xxiv. 14.
[5] Rom. xv. 9.

their temples were abandoned.[1] "We are but of yesterday," says Tertullian at the end of the second century,[2] "and yet we occupy your whole land, the cities and islands, the camp, palace, Senate, and Forum; we have left you nothing but your temples." "There exists not any country," says St. Justin, "wherein prayers are not offered to the Universal Father through Jesus Christ crucified."[3]

Such is the witness of prophecy, and the voice is still heard. Revelation must be always prophetic, for the salvation it promises is only to be accomplished in the future, and each age has with the revelation as thus far fulfilled its own special warnings. The fulfilment of the Messianic prophecies in Christ imposed on Israel the obligation of believing in Him, and so Christians who have witnessed the accomplishment of His prophecies in His Church, are bound with rekindled faith and hope to expect His final Advent, of which the doom of Israel was the type, and His living Church the promise.

"That the Catholic Church," says Bossuet, "fills all preceding centuries in continuity is an indisputable fact. The Law precedes the Gospel; the succession of Moses and the Patriarchs is one and the same with that of Jesus Christ. The mark of the Messias in whom we believe, is that He was expected, and came, and was acknowledged by a never-ending posterity— Jesus Christ, yesterday, to-day, and for all ages. Four or five authentic facts, clear as daylight, show our

[1] *Ep.*, lib. x. c. 97. [2] *Apolog.*, c. 37. [3] *Dial. c. Tryphon*, c. 117.

religion to be as ancient as the world itself. Therefore they prove that it had no other author than the Creator of the Universe, in whose hand are all things, and who alone could begin and carry out a scheme which embraces all ages." [1]

[1] *Hist. Univ.*, ii. fin.

CHAPTER VII

CHRIST AND CHRISTIANITY

IN the preceding chapters Christianity has been considered as the new birth of a corrupt and decaying world, a new order of things in every sphere and relation of human life. Nearly two thousand years have elapsed since the face of the world was thus transformed, and they have been two thousand years of conflict. The sophistry of heathenism, backed by Pagan Rome; the heresies of the Middle Ages, allied with imperial and feudal tyrants; false philosophy, the revolt of the human intellect against tradition and authority, with its consequent results, anarchy and the new Cæsarism—such have been the foes encountered by Christianity. Yet it has survived. What is its origin and the secret of its strength?

Gibbon, and, after him, Strauss and others, have attributed the spread of Christianity to purely natural causes. The Handbooks, now so common, on the —so-called—science of religion, profess to show in detail how Christianity is, like Buddhism and Mahommedanism, a modification of pre-existing creeds, another purely human development in the history of religious thought. We will examine in detail some of these alleged "Christian origins."

First, the political condition of the civilised world, as it then was, is assigned as one chief cause of the rapid diffusion of Christianity. All nations were united under the paternal government of Rome, and every freeborn subject, of whatever race, could claim the right and privileges of a Roman citizen. Further, there was the rapidity of communication effected by the magnificent roads, the invariable sign of Rome's extended sway. And lastly, there was the facility of intercourse afforded by unity of language, the Latin tongue prevailing through the Western, the Greek through the Eastern provinces of the Empire. All this, it is said, suffices in great part to account for the spread of the Christian religion.

Again, the philosophies current during the first ages of the Church are said to have prepared the ground for Christianity. Philo, for instance, taught the Platonic doctrine of the Logos, and the whole school of Alexandrian Judaism had familiarised men's minds with the idea of the Incarnation. The Oriental cults and Judaism paved the way for sacrifice and priesthood; Polytheism, for the intercession of the Blessèd Virgin and the Saints. As regards its ethical code, Celsus found the teaching of Plato superior to that of Christ, just as the maxims of Marcus Aurelius are compared in our own day with those of the Gospel, and Seneca is coupled with St. Paul. Nay, more, the Neo-Platonists could present, under the figure of Apollonius, a leader and saviour of men, in word and work greater than Christ. He, too, was more than mortal, a reformer of heathenism, a severe ascetic, a model of every virtue, a teacher of heavenly wisdom, by miracles and prophecy approving himself divine. Christianity, then, was but one phase of the religious impulse which manifested itself at that time.

Now, Christian writers from the first have recognised the intellectual and political condition of the world at the advent of Christ as preordained for that event. He "came in the fulness of time," and the unity of government, citizenship, and language, and the diffusion in various ways of the Messianic idea, assisted, doubtless, the work of the apostolic missions. But are these favourable circumstances alone sufficient to account for the effect which followed? If so, why did they operate so powerfully only in favour of Christianity, and fail so completely as regards the other systems, philosophical or religious, then rife, and which were promulgated under precisely the same conditions? Why were heathen sage and heresiarch leader forgotten in a generation, while Christianity lived? "Cur, O delirium caput nemo Apollonium pro Deo colit?" Lactantius could write, only a century after the false Christ had died.

These causes are then insufficient to account for the effect produced—the rise, spread, and vitality of the Christian religion. Nor can it be explained but as the work of Christ. Who then was Christ?

How did He appear outwardly to the heathen world? A Jew, born of poor parents in an obscure province of the Empire, and belonging to a hated race. When He began to speak, after thirty years of seclusion and toil, His kinsfolk thought Him mad, for He was but "the carpenter's son," and "had learnt no letters." Nor was there anything striking or extraordinary as His public life advanced. His teaching contained no new thought on the ideas current at the time, philosophical or political—nothing that men looked for in a great Teacher. His words were simple, spoken as the occasion demanded, without art, eloquence, or preparation, to this or that individual, to a crowd of poor and ignorant people, or to a group of Scribes and Pharisees learned in the law. All places were the same to Him—the sick chamber or the crowded synagogue, the mountain-side or the Temple portico. Yet these simple words revealed sublime mysteries—the inner life of God, of Father, Son, and Spirit; they taught a justice exceeding that of the Scribes and Pharisees, a purity embracing the whole mind and heart, a desire for perfection infinite and divine.

As His teaching was simple, so His actions were devoid of singularity. He was accessible to all. Crowds pressed on Him by day; at night He would instruct those, like Nicodemus, afraid of seeking Him before men. He invited all to draw near, especially the weary and heavy-laden in body and soul; to all alike He gave rest, not the impotent sympathy of human consolation, but new life of flesh and spirit.

He bore with all, the dulness and petulance of His disciples, the taunts and questioning of His enemies; of all He was the servant, He came " not to be ministered to, but to minister."

What return, then, did He meet with after doing all things well? The ideal just man, according to Plato, must prove his justice by leaving all for justice' sake. Though innocent, he must be calumniated, scourged, tortured, and put to death; and all this he will bear unmoved because he desires not to appear just, but to be so. But the ideal was never realised. Cicero said, "Philosophy has shown us what the perfect man ought to be, but I have never seen one."[1] In Jesus Christ the perfect man was found, and in suffering His perfection was manifested. The fanatic is unconscious of tortures in devotion to his cause; the Stoic regards pain with indifference because it is inevitable. But Christ felt His sufferings in their fulness, and endured them of His own free will. From the first He was a man of sorrows, and acquainted with grief; He had felt hunger and thirst; He had spent years as a homeless, friendless, wandering outcast, exposed to insult and calumny and bodily danger; and it was with a life-long experience of pain and sorrow, and with every sense and feeling active and energetic within Him, that He entered on His passion alone, and endured it to the end. " He was led as a lamb to the slaughter, and as a sheep before his shearers is dumb, so opened He not His mouth."

[1] *Qu. Tusc.*, ii. 22, 31.

This the prophet foretold, and this Christ accomplished.

The treachery of His disciples, the perjury of the false witnesses, the insults of His judges, the physical torments, the blasphemies of the whole people, the desertion of the Apostles, the dereliction by His Father, were borne in silence, or only elicited a prayer for His murderers.

A comparison has been at times attempted between the death of Socrates and of Christ. In what does it consist? "The one drank with grace the poisonous draught, conscious that, though hated by a few, he enjoyed the regard of his fellow-citizens and the tender affection of his disciples. The other drains to the dregs a chalice of unparalleled suffering, outraged and insulted by His whole nation, abandoned and betrayed by His dearest followers. What a contrast in their manner! The one, supported by his numerous friends, defends himself with earnestness and ingenuity, perhaps even with the sacrifice of his principles, and beguiles his last moments by the cheering speculations of his profession. The other, though innocent, stands mute through His various trials, and remains calm and equable under torture and desolation. Yet the silence of Christ convinced Pilate, while the eloquence of the sage failed to move his judges. Finally, Socrates makes the dramatic exit, becoming a philosopher, while in the eyes of the centurion and the multitude Christ died as a God."[1]

What, then, was the purpose of His life and death?

[1] Wiseman's Sermons, *Christ in His Passion*, abbreviated.

He came to do His Father's will, to seek and save that which was lost. The whole world was in sin, and He alone could save it. No human mind has ever conceived a thought so divine—*For all men Heaven always.* How was it to be accomplished? Only by Himself. "I am the Way, the Truth, and the Life." The world was in darkness. He alone was the light. He was the true light, because, though born of a woman, He was the Eternal Son of God. He was the one atoning sacrifice for sin, because the shame, pain, and death, endured in His human nature, were of infinite value through its union with the Divine Person, and as an oblation of His infinite love. As God-man, in Him are reconciled apparently contradictory attributes, and the seeming paradox of Christian doctrine and Christian life is solved. Though laden with the guilt of the world, He could challenge His enemies to convince Him of sin. Without comeliness, He was the most beautiful among the sons of men. He ministers as a servant, while He declared Himself equal with God; without study, He knew all things. He is weak at the prospect of death, strong when He meets it face to face. He opens Paradise to the penitent thief, and descends Himself to hell. He is Viator and Comprehensor, a traveller on earth's pilgrimage, yet from the first in the Father's bosom. He is born and He dies, yet is He the "Pater futuri sæculi"—Father of the world to come—and He lives in all time. He comes of one particular race and family, yet is He the Exemplar of every human life.

And that which makes Him, infinite though He be alike in His grandeur and His lowliness, an object of love and of imitation for all, was that very self-sacrifice which is His guiding principle in life and death. Neither His Wisdom nor His Power, neither His Parables nor His Miracles, nor even the Incarnation itself, is the one absorbing thought of the Apostle's mind, but rather the single fact that God had died for him. The beginning and end of his faith was that Jesus, "having joy set before Him, endured the Cross." Hence he will know nothing else but Christ and Him crucified, and he prays God that he may never glory save in the Cross of his Lord.

So, too, the preaching of the Apostles was not merely the doctrine of Christ, nor His system of morals, but His life and acts, and, above all, His death. "Christ also suffered for us, leaving you an example, that you should follow in His steps." The Christian was to put on Jesus Christ. He was to be clothed anew; the life of Christ was to be manifested in his flesh without; within, he was to aim at reproducing in himself, in mind and will, what Christ had thought and felt. And if, on the one hand, the convert was called upon to leave home, goods, friends, and life itself, yet such sacrifice, impossible to human nature, was accomplished in the grace of Christ, by which he passed from the servitude of corruption to the liberty and glory of the sons of God. What though he had lost all, still he had found all; the saints were his brethren, God his Father, and heaven his home.

THE FIRST CHRISTIANS

This was the Lever which moved the world, and alone explains the change which followed, the reproduction of Christ in the lives of His followers. In His name they measured their weakness against the power of this world and the gates of hell. By the sign of the Cross they healed the sick, cast out devils, and paralysed the Pagan magicians. But their faith and its attendant gifts were not for their own glorification, but to save the souls for whom Christ died. Thus every Christian became an apostle, and by his new life of purity, humility, patience, even more than by his miraculous powers, the glad tidings were communicated. The father converted his child, the soldier his comrade, the slave his master. In that heathen world the Christian community appeared as a new-born race. Amidst the multiplying sects of human creeds and philosophies, they owned one faith, obeyed one law, recognised one Head; and while selfishness and greed set class against class, and man against man, the Christians of every race or condition were of one heart and one soul. In an age, too, when high and low bowed down before the tyrant of the day, the Christian alone, while second to none in his civil loyalty, fearlessly asserted his spiritual freedom, and that his soul belonged to God alone. " Solius autem Dei homo."

And the efforts of its persecutors only gave new strength to the Infant Church. The constancy of the martyrs is often named as one cause of the spread of Christianity. But the heathen world was accustomed at the gladiatorial shows to see men die by thousands, and meet death with indifference. Yet, while the stricken athlete was the sculptor's model in the grace, dignity, and fortitude of his last moments, the Christian martyr was a spectacle to God, to angels, and to men. A gentle patience, beyond the power of his persecutors to disturb, a divine charity manifested by prayer for his murderers, a faith and hope so keen as to see the Heavens opened, and the life of glory begun, such were the characteristics of the Christian martyr, and with every martyrdom the Standard of the Crucified was planted anew. "Christianus, qui Christi est," says St. Gregory, and this the world saw.

Lastly, let us briefly consider the two systems, the Mahomedan and the Buddhist, by some supposed to be the rivals of Christianity. It has been already stated (Chapter II.) that all men recognise, by reason alone, certain natural virtues; and further, that every creed shows some traces—though terribly obscured and corrupted—of the primal revelation still remaining. The characteristics of a religion are then to be found, not in what each has in common with the other, but in what is exclusively its own, not where it agrees with other systems, but where it differs.

Now the truths which Christ, and Christ alone, made known to the world, furnished a wholly supernatural knowledge of God, His nature and attributes, as revealed in Christ Himself, angelic purity of life, and an inward holiness to be attained only by God's grace and for God's sake, with Heaven as its reward. Mahomet claimed also to bring a revelation from Heaven. In common with Judaism, and with the Arian and other Eastern heresies, he taught the unity of God, and with them he too denied the Incarnation. Christ was only a Prophet, and one too of a series completed in Mahomet himself. His moral code teaches, in common again with Judaism, prayer, fasting, and almsgiving; but authorises, under a professedly divine revelation, polygamy, and an unlimited concubinage. His religion was to be spread by force, "the sword and the swords of God;" its final end is in name heaven; but the paradise of Mahomet consisted in an immense Harem, surrounded by gardens of brilliant colours, and fragrant with many scented flowers.

Of the success of Mahomet and the number of his followers, Pascal says, "Any man could do what Mahomet did, for he wrought no miracles, he was confirmed by no prophecies. No man could do what Jesus did. Mahomet slew, Jesus Christ caused His own to be slain. In fact, the two systems are so contrary, that if Mahomet took the way, humanly speaking, to succeed, Jesus Christ, humanly speaking, took the way to perish. And instead of concluding from Mahomet's success that Jesus Christ might well have succeeded, we should rather say that since Mahomet succeeded, Jesus Christ ought to have perished."

The chief points of the Buddhist religion can be

considered under the heads already named. Primitive Buddhism recognised no Personal God, it was in fact a purely atheistic system. Instead of doctrinal teaching, it encouraged metaphysical speculations about substance and matter, all tending to blank scepticism. The various legendary dogmas and deities, together with their worship and ritual, now found in popular Buddhism, are subsequent additions; and the worship of these deities in a religion which has no definite knowledge of God, often tends to simple idolatry. The essence of the whole system " revealed " to Buddha under the Bo tree was as follows. Pain comes from existence, existence from the desire of possessing it. The perfect annihilation, not only of the passions, but of every human or natural inclination, emancipates the soul from the misery of existence, and leads to Nirvana or extinction; "it is extinguished as the light of a lamp." The soul not fit for Nirvana must be further purified by being born again in gods, animals, and evil spirits, till by this metempsychosis it arrives in time at annihilation. Buddhism retains certain precepts of the decalogue, but it is morality without dogma, religion without God. It knows nothing of faith, redemption, grace; its only means are unaided human effort, and its end, not eternal life with our Father in Heaven, but extinction in the absolute nothingness.

To sum up, then, we have found that what non-Christian religions have that is true is found in Christianity, what is exclusively their own is false.

Their rise, spread, and duration are all referable to natural causes, conquest, state policy, affinity of race or speech; when these causes fail, they too expire. Christianity alone can be traced to no human origin, and is explicable only as the work of Christ. That work was predicted in a series of ages before He came, and was fulfilled by Him alone. It was confirmed by physical miracles, wrought by Himself and His Apostles, and is perpetuated in the moral miracle, the existence of His One Holy Catholic Church. Through Christ, as taught by her, we obtain the only true knowledge of God and of ourselves. Through His sufferings we learn the malice of sin and the depth of our own misery. Through His Resurrection we learn the omnipotence of God and the Infinitude of His Divine Mercy. But Christ is now and always "signum contradictionis" for the rise and fall of many. He is hidden from the wise and prudent, but revealed only to babes. To the unbeliever, whether Gentile or Jew, He is a scandal and folly. But the Revelation of God in Christ, to those who receive it, is a new and supernatural life begun on earth, to be consummated in Heaven. And that this new life in Christ is not a figure of speech, but a living reality, and that the faith works miracles, may be seen in the testimony of one who shed his blood for confessing Christ. The experience of Cyprian, the fiery martyr of the African Church, is repeated in the consciousness of every Christian soul who has passed from darkness to light and is faithful to the grace received. "When," he says, "I lay in darkness and in that blind night of ignorance, whilst I floated hither and thither, as doubtful and wavering in the sea of this troublesome world, being ignorant of my own life, and void both of truth and light, I did esteem it hard and difficult, according to these manners of mine, that which God's mercy did promise for my salvation; a new life through baptism, newness of body and soul, and this, notwithstanding my former corruption, and while still in the same flesh. This, I say, seemed to me impossible; for how, said I to myself, can so great a conversion be expected, how can that which by continuance has been made, as it were, natural and immovably engrafted, be on a sudden shaken off? How can a man, said I to myself, delicately fed and pampered, learn parsimony and abstinence, or exchange gold and purple for mean attire, the pomp and insignia of rule and power for a rude and humble obscurity. How can a man, once entangled in the snares and alluring baits of vice, securely master the cravings of intemperance, the elation of pride, the fire of anger, the restlessness of greed, the sting of cruelty, the lures of ambition, the tyranny of rebellious lust. Thus did I debate with myself before my conversion, so that my amendment seemed hopeless. But after that the Holy Ghost, coming from above, did renew me by a second Nativity, making me a new man, it is wonderful how soon those things which were doubtful before, were made clear, and those things opened which before were shut; and those things did shine which before were dusky and dark, it is wonderful, I say, how that which seemed hard, was now made easy, and what I thought impossible, was now within my power."[1]

[1] Cyprian, L. T. C. I., abridged from trans. F. Parsons, S.J., Christ direct, part ii. chap. ii. p. 460.

APPENDIX

[For the following Appendix the Editor is indebted to the Rev. HENRY CATOR, of the London Oratory.]

THE TÜBINGEN THEORY [1]

SINCE the time of Ferdinand C. Baur, the founder of the Tübingen School, who died in 1844, the authenticity of the Canonical Gospels has been constantly attacked by the rationalist writers of this school of criticism. The only point of agreement arrived at by these critics seems to be that the Synoptic Gospels, though earlier than that of St. John, are, in their present form, in great measure the work of authors other than those named by tradition, and that the Fourth Gospel is not the work of the Apostle St. John. As to the dates at which these Gospels were composed, the widest difference of opinion prevails, as will be seen by the following table:—

	St. Matthew.	St. Mark.	St. Luke.	St. John.
	A.D.	A.D.	A.D.	A.D.
Baur	130-134	After St. Matthew	About 100	150-170
Hilgenfeld	80	Before 100	Before 120	About 150
Keim	65-70	About 100	After 70	98-117
Holtzmann	69-96	Between 69-96	96-117	100-140
Renan	Discourses, about 45	After 67	After 70	95-100

[1] Dr. Lightfoot's dissertation on "St. Paul and the Three" has been largely made use of in the following chapter.

Renan, it should be noticed, considers that the discourses of our Lord in St. Matthew's Gospel are authentic, but maintains that the narrative portion is by a later hand, and is probably based upon St. Mark's Gospel. He sees no reason to doubt the traditional authorship of the Second and Third Gospels, while the Fourth Gospel, in his judgment, is based on an authentic work of St. John, and was published by his disciples at the end of the first century. It will be remarked that the earlier dates assigned by Keim, Holtzmann, and Renan, are all of them consistent with the traditional authorship. Catholic and conservative critics would date St. Matthew's Aramaic original between 42 and 67 A.D., and the Greek translation 67–80 A.D., St. Mark's Gospel not later than 67 A.D., St. Luke's not later than 80 A.D., and St. John's 90–100 A.D. Thus there is but little discrepancy between the more moderate critics of the Modern Tübingen School and orthodox writers as to the dating of the Canonical Gospels. There is, however, a wide diversity of opinion between them as to the authority assigned to these Gospels in the Church from the time of their publication up to the latter portion of the second century. The Tübingen School asserts that up to the date of the Muratorian Canon (170–180 A.D.), or of Irenæus (175 A.D.), or of Clement of Alexandria (170–220 A.D.), or of Tertullian (170–240 A.D.), or at least before 160 or 170 A.D., other Gospels, that according to the Hebrews, of Peter, and some others now lost, similar, indeed, in context to the Canonical Gospels,

PETRINE AND PAULINE PARTIES 189

and yet distinct from them, were considered as of equal or even greater authority. Further, we are told that somewhere about the second half of the second century, out of a mass of Evangelical literature, the Church selected our four Gospels, stamped them with Canonical authority, and assigned them to St. Matthew, St. Mark, St. Luke, and St. John. Henceforth these Gospels were received as divinely inspired and authoritative records of our Lord's life and ministry, and the other Gospels sank into obscurity and disuse. It is further said that not one of the Gospels, Canonical or Uncanonical, remains in its original form, but all of them were modified, altered, and added to, in order to conform them to the various phases of dogmatic development—the Canonical Gospels in the interests of Catholic Ecclesiasticism, and the Gospel according to the Hebrews, and the Pseudo-Peter, in the interests of the heretical sects who made use of them. Hence it is the work of criticism to discriminate between the original document—the proto-Matthew or proto-Mark—and the additions made for doctrinal reasons.

According to this theory, the Church, during the Apostolic age, and for two or three generations later, was divided into antagonistic parties. St. Peter, St. James, and St. John were the leaders of the Jewish party. St. Paul was the founder and leader of the so-called Pauline party. These two parties were as opposed to one another as the Ritualists and the Evangelicals in the Church of England. At last, however, a fusion was effected by mutual concessions, which resulted in the birth of the Catholic Church, and the selection and adaptation of the Gospels to suit the new form of Christianity. The Petrine Gospel of Matthew was modified in a Pauline sense, the colourless Second Gospel (of Mark), and the Third Gospel and the Acts, both conciliatory in tendency, were attributed respectively to Mark the disciple of St. Peter, and Luke the disciple of Paul, while the strongly anti-Jewish and theological Fourth Gospel, at a later date, was assigned to St. John. St. Peter and St. Paul, who had been, according to this theory, bitterly opposed in life, were now represented as the joint founders of the Roman Church. The true disciples of St. Peter, the Ebionites, sank into the obscurity of an insignificant sect, while the extreme Pauline School, as represented by Marcion, was formally excommunicated. Thus it was, we are told, through the influence of a conciliatory party that the Catholic Church was formed towards the close of the second century.

Such is the latest "scientific" account of the origin of the Church and her Gospels. But strange to say, the whole of this revolution which must have shaken Christianity to its very foundations, passed unnoticed in history, and was absolutely unknown and unheard of by men like Irenæus, Clement, and Tertullian, whose immediate predecessors lived in the midst of the conflict. It can readily be shown that such representations are at variance with the facts related in the

Acts of the Apostles, and in the passages bearing on St. Paul's relations with St. Peter, St. James, and St. John in the four Epistles of St. Paul (received as genuine even by the extreme left of the Tübingen School), and are equally at variance with the facts narrated i.. the historical records of the first and second centuries.

What, then, are the facts. St. Paul was most emphatic in declaring that he received both his Apostolate and his doctrine not from men or through men, but directly from God and Christ. Nevertheless, in order to silence the opposition of the Hebraic Christians, who questioned his authority, he went up to Jerusalem to see Peter, stayed with him fifteen days, and at the same time saw James, the brother of the Lord, who was Bishop of Jerusalem. After fifteen years, in obedience to a revelation, he went again to Jerusalem, together with Barnabas and Titus, for the express purpose of comparing the Gospel he preached with those who were Apostles before him, and who alone were esteemed authorities by the Judaising party, "Lest perhaps," he says, "I should run, or had run in vain."[1] The result of this conference was that nothing was found wanting in Paul's doctrine. His Apostolate was recognised. Titus, who was a Gentile, was not required to be circumcised. "And when they had known the grace that was given to me" (Paul), "James and Cephas and John, who seemed to be pillars, gave to me and Barnabas the right hands of fellowship, that we should go unto the Gentiles and they unto the

[1] Gal. ii. 2.

circumcision."[1] From St. Paul we learn a further fact —that St. Peter held himself free to observe or not observe the Jewish law according to circumstances and expediency, and that he was blamed by St. Paul, not for becoming with the Jews a Jew, and with the Gentiles a Gentile, but for misusing, according to St. Paul's judgment, his Christian liberty, so as to appear to lend his great authority to those who wished to impose the observance of the law on the Gentile converts of Antioch, a course of conduct prejudicial to the brotherly understanding hitherto existing between them and the Hebrew Christians of that place. "Before some came from James he did eat with the Gentiles: but when they were come, he withdrew and separated himself, fearing them who were of the circumcision, and to his dissimulation the rest of the Jews consented, so that Barnabas also was led by these into that dissimulation."[2] That this quarrel was not doctrinal, and produced no permanent rupture between the two Apostles, is shown by St. Paul's claim to rank with the chiefest Apostles, those that are above measure Apostles;[3] by the first Epistle of Peter, which is rejected, in the teeth of ample external evidence, simply because it is markedly Pauline in its tone and doctrine; and by the evidence of those who were immediate disciples of the Apostles, and succeeded them in their government of the Church. If the Tübingen theory were true, there must necessarily have been violent controversies and dissensions between the rival parties

[1] Gal. ii. 9.   [2] Gal. ii. 12, 13.   [3] 2 Cor. xii. 11.

formed on the one side by the teaching of Peter, James, and John, and on the other by Paul and Barnabas. If Peter and Paul were as much opposed to each other, as say, St. Ignatius of Loyola and Luther, and opposed not on minor questions, but on their doctrine, regarding the Person of Christ and the means of salvation, the Church would have been rent asunder, and vehement protests from either side would have followed. Asia Minor, the home of St. John during his latter years, would have been at enmity with Rome, and with the other Churches now under the influence of St. Paul. Palestine, the centre of Judaic Christianity, and Jerusalem, the See of St. James, would have ranged their forces against Corinth and Rome. The Church of Gaul, then apparently closely connected with Asia Minor, would have been disunited from Rome and the West. Finally, the disciples of Peter would be found in open conflict with the disciples of Paul, the School of St. John dissociated from the Pauline Churches of Philippi and Rome, the Church of Rome itself divided into two antagonistic sects.

But what do we find? Instead of Peter and Paul being regarded as leaders of contending parties, in the Epistle of Clement of Rome (97 A.D.) both Apostles are spoken of together as "the greatest and most just pillars of the Church," "the illustrious Apostles," "noble examples."[1] The Corinthians are bidden "Take up the Epistle of the blessed Paul the Apostle, in truth he spiritually charged you concerning him-

[1] *Ep. ad. Cor. I.*, cap. 5.

self, and Cephas, and Apollo."[1] In this Epistle Pauline doctrine is combined with reverence for Jewish institutions—the Temple and the Sacrifices; the Christian hierarchy is compared to that of the Jews; the language of the Epistles of Peter and James is interwoven with that of Paul; the virtues and martyrdom of SS. Peter and Paul are praised as of "men who spent their lives in the practice of holiness." When we come to Ignatius of Antioch (103 A.D.), an uncompromising opponent of Judaic tendencies, it is the same. In his letter to the Church of Rome he writes: "I do not command you like Peter and Paul —they were Apostles; while I am a condemned man."[2] Again, Polycarp, the disciple of St. John, who, therefore, according to the rationalist critics, ought to have been extremely anti-Pauline, writes to the Pauline Church of Philippi: "The blessed and glorious Paul wrote letters to you, into which if you look diligently, you will be able to be built up in the faith given to you."[3] This Epistle of Polycarp is scarcely more than a network of phrases and expressions derived from the First Epistle of St. Peter and the Pauline Epistles, including the Pastoral Epistles, while there are two plain and remarkable coincidences with the First Epistle of St. John.[4] But this is not all. Polycarp in his old age undertook a journey to Rome to consult with Anicetus the Pope on the Paschal question, the one controversy, as far as we know,

---

[1] *Ep. ad. Cor. I.*, cap. 49.
[2] *Ep. ad. Rom.* 4.
[3] *Ep. ad. Philipp.* 3.
[4] *Ibid.*, cap. 7, 8.

which disturbed the internal peace of the Church at this period. The Pope maintained the Roman custom of observing the anniversaries of our Lord's Passion always on Friday, while Polycarp pleaded the authority of St. John for observing it on 14th Nisan, irrespective of the day of the week. Neither changed their custom, and a toleration of the diverse usages was finally agreed upon; while in token of unity of faith and Christian charity, the Pope received the Holy Eucharist at the hands of Polycarp. Irenæus, the disciple of Polycarp, speaking of this incident, remarks that diversity of usage only serves to show the unity of the faith, and tells us that his Master preached in Rome, converted heretics, and denounced Marcion as the first-born of Satan.

About the same time (150 A.D.), during the Pontificate of Anicetus, whose deacon Eleutherius was Pope when Irenæus wrote, Hegesippus, a Hebrew Christian of Jerusalem, journeyed from Palestine to Rome. He was, as may be seen from the extracts from his five books of Memoirs, preserved by Eusebius, a thorough Hebrew in national feelings and cast of mind, but like St. Paul, who was a Hebrew of the Hebrews, Hegesippus was no Ebionite. On his way he conversed with the bishops of the various cities through which he passed, and he gives us the following account of his experiences. "And the Church of Corinth," he says, "continued in the true faith until Primus was bishop there, with whom I had familiar conversation, as I passed many days at Corinth, when I was sailing to Rome, during which time we were mutually refreshed in the true principles. After coming to Rome, I made my stay with Anicetus, whose deacon was Eleutherius. After Anicetus, Soter succeeded, and after him, Eleutherius. In every succession, and in every city, the doctrine prevails according to what is taught in the law, the Prophets and the Lord.[1] As to his doctrine, Eusebius, who had his five books of Memoirs before him,[2] gives the clearest testimony to his Catholicity. He speaks of him as "having recorded the unerring tradition of the Apostolic preaching." He names him together with Dionysius of Corinth, Pinytus, Philip, Apollinaris, Melito, Musanus, Modestus, and Irenæus, "whose correct views of the sound faith have descended to us in the works written by them, as they received it from Apostolic tradition," and says that he "left the fullest record of his opinions in five books of Memoirs." We find Hegesippus, by his own testimony, in cordial relations with the Churches along his route to Rome, with the Bishop of Corinth, a Church claiming to be founded, like that of Rome, by Peter and Paul, as we see from the Epistle of Dionysius to Pope Soter. Certainly Hegesippus was not an Ebionite, unless the whole Church was Ebionite also. This we know was not the case. But lest it should seem as though we were suppressing anything that tells against our conclusion regarding his Catholicity, it should be noticed that it is said that Hegesippus condemned the words, "Eye hath not seen," &c., as

[1] H. E., iv. 22. [2] H. E., iv. 21.

contradicting the words of our Lord, " Blessed are your eyes, for ye see," &c. It is contended that this shows hi santi-Paulinism. But it should be observed—First, these words are quoted in the Epistle of Clement, which he met with, and apparently read with approval, at Corinth. Secondly, in 1 Cor. ii., where they occur, they are quoted by St. Paul from the Old Testament (Isa. lxiv. 4), and therefore it is most improbable that as a Hebrew, Hegesippus should find fault with them in themselves. Thirdly, we know from Hippolytus that the words were used in certain Gnostic forms of initiation, and it was to a false use of the words, not to the words themselves, therefore, that Hegesippus objected.

Justin Martyr, like Hegesippus, was a native of Palestine, but was by birth a Samaritan. His writings prove that he was well acquainted with the Epistles of St. Paul, for he makes frequent and unmistakable use of the Apostle's language, and his quotations from the Old Testament in many cases agree with St. Paul, where the latter differs from the Hebrew and Septuagint. Now Justin explicitly condemns Ebionism, both as regards its doctrine on the Person of Christ, and the obligation of the Law, for he doubts whether those who maintain its universal obligation can be saved.[1] Now, Justin was acquainted with the doctrine of the Church at Ephesus, where (132–135 A.D.) he held his controversy with Trypho, and the Church of Rome, where he lived until his martyrdom.

[1] *Dial.* 47, 48, 127.

It only remains to consider the relations which subsisted between the Churches of Gaul and Asia Minor on the one hand, and the Church of Rome on the other. Irenæus was by birth and bringing up an Asiatic.[1] He was a disciple of Polycarp, whose teaching he treasured up in his mind and followed in his doctrine. Besides Polycarp, he knew and quotes other Presbyters and Elders,[2] who were disciples of the elder Apostles, and especially of St. John. He quotes also from Papias, who, he asserts, was a companion of Polycarp, a hearer of John. He evidently was unaware of any antagonism between the schools of St. John and St. Paul, for in a quotation from "the Elders, the disciples of the Apostles," he represents them as using words of the Fourth Gospel and the First Epistle to the Corinthians.[3] Moreover, he succeeded in the Episcopate of Lyons, Pothinus, who died about 177 A.D., at the advanced age of ninety years; and since Pothinus was probably an Asiatic, and was born some ten years before the death of St. John, Irenæus was connected by yet another link with the Apostolic age, and was the inheritor of independent traditions through Pothinus, under whom he was a presbyter at Lyons, before he himself became Bishop. Hitherto we have considered Irenæus only in relation to the Asiatic School of St. John, in which he received his early training, and with which he kept up connection, as we see by the Epistle of the Churches of Lyons and

---

[1] Euseb., H. E., v. 20.   [2] Iren., *Adv. Hær.*, v. 33.
[3] *Hær.*, v. 12, 36.

Vienne,[1] written about 177 A.D. to those brethren in Asia and Phrygia having the same faith and hope with them. If the School of John was Ebionite and anti-Pauline, certainly we should expect Irenæus to display these tendencies. Now, we must consider the relations in which he stood with Rome and the rest of the Catholic Church. Nothing can be more fatal to the Tübingen hypothesis than the testimony of Irenæus on this point. Imbued as he was with Asiatic traditions, educated in a country which is associated with the teaching not only of St. John but also of St. Andrew and St. Philip, and perhaps other Apostles who seem after the destruction of Jerusalem to have made Asia Minor their headquarters, appealing throughout his life to the doctrine of the Presbyters, the disciples of the Apostles of the Circumcision, himself Presbyter first, and afterwards Bishop of a Church probably of Asiatic origin, but certainly in close and constant communication with the " School of St. John,"—if Judaising Ebionitic Christianity were the characteristic features of this school, we should surely expect to find Irenæus an Ebionite. Facts, however, emphatically contradict this supposition. His writings teem with quotations from the Pauline Epistles. He accepts as divinely inspired not only the Gospel of St. Matthew, but those of St. Mark, St. Luke, and St. John.[2] He, and the Church of which he was Bishop, observe the Paschal feast according to the Roman usage, though at the

[1] Euseb., H. E., v. 1. [2] Ibid., v. 24.

same time he remonstrates with Pope Victor for hastily threatening to excommunicate the Asiatic Churches for following their ancient tradition in this matter. Further, Irenæus had the most profound reverence for the See of Rome. He speaks of it as "the greatest, the most ancient and universally known Church, founded and constituted at Rome by the two most glorious Apostles Peter and Paul."[1] He says it would be a long and tedious task to enumerate the successions of all the Churches, and indeed is unnecessary, for "the faith announced to all men, which through the succession of her (Rome's) Bishops has come down to us," is, as a matter of fact, the faith of all the Churches, and necessarily so, "for with this Church, on account of her more powerful headship (propter potiorem principalitatem), it is necessary that every Church, that is, the faithful everywhere dispersed, should agree (convenire), in which Church has always been preserved that tradition, which is from the Apostles." The importance of this testimony of Irenæus cannot be overrated. His faith, he asserts, in the face of Catholics and heretics, is the faith of Polycarp, the faith of St. John the Apostle, and at the same time the faith of Rome and the whole Church. Each link of the chain is supported by a body of independent evidence, the identity of the faith of Polycarp with that of St. John, by the Presbyters, the disciples of the Apostles; the identity of Polycarp's faith with that of Irenæus and the whole Church

[1] *Hær.*, iii. 3.

of his age, by the testimony of the later Asiatic Church, the See of Rome, and the succession of the apostolically founded Churches throughout the world. And that his faith was Catholic, not exclusively Petrine or Pauline in the sense of the Tübingen School, we know with the highest degree of certainty from his writings and those of his contemporaries. Thus, through the testimony of the Apostles Peter and Paul themselves; through Clement, Ignatius, and Polycarp, the disciples of the Apostles; through Hegesippus and Justin, both Christians of Palestine in the earlier portion of the second century; and through Irenæus, the Churches of Gaul, and Asia Minor in the end of the second century, we have traced the unity of faith and continuity of doctrine which existed throughout the Churches most closely connected with the Apostles Peter, Paul, John, and James the Bishop of Jerusalem, up to the end of the second century, when the Church was undoubtedly not Petrine or Pauline but Catholic.

The evidence which has been given for the Catholicity of the Church from its very foundation by the Apostles, *may* no doubt be set aside by arbitrary hypothesis. The authors of the Acts of the Apostles, and the First and Second Epistles of St. Peter; Clement of Rome, Ignatius, Polycarp, and Hegesippus *may* be represented as belonging to a Conciliatory School, who sought to combine the Petrine and Pauline parties into which the Church in its earlier stages was divided. Ebionism, on the one hand, and Marcionism, on the other, *may* be represented as survivals of the primitive state of Christianity, and Catholicism as the outcome of the mediation of a Conciliatory School. The Epistle of Barnabas, dated variously between 90 and 120 A.D., with its violent anti-Judaic tendency, and the Clementine Homilies, the work of an Essene Judaiser of Gnostic tendencies about 150 A.D., *may* be pronounced typical products of Pauline and strongly anti-Pauline schools respectively, rather than the extreme opinions of an isolated individual in the case of Barnabas, and of an adherent of a waning sect in the case of the author of the Clementines. The fact *may* be ignored that the name of Peter was invoked to back up anti-Judaic opinions, by Basilides (130 A.D.), who claimed to have been taught by Glaucias, an "interpreter of Peter;" by the writer of the so-called Preaching of Peter; and by the Apocryphal Gospel of Peter, docetic, and strongly anti-Judaic in its tendency—all probably of as early a date as the Clementines; yet we cannot but think that if truth be sought rather than ingenious theories, St. Paul himself and his disciple St. Luke, the personal disciples of the Apostles, holding important posts of authority in the Church, and the representatives of Palestine and Asia Minor in the following age, ought to be preferred as witnesses to the author of the Clementines and the writer of the Epistle to Barnabas. Of these two, the author of the Clementines felt the opinion of Christendom so strongly set against him, that he dared not attack Paul openly, but only in a veiled manner under the name of Simon Magus; and the writer of the Epistle of Barnabas was an overzealous opponent of the Judaisers, whose opinions are unsupported save perhaps partially by later writers of the Alexandrian School. If the so-called Conciliatory School was not a mere party in the Church, but the School of the Apostles, Petrine as well as Pauline, because it represented the united teaching of Peter and Paul, who recognised one another's Apostolic authority, and worked together in unity of Faith and brotherly Charity, then the conclusion follows that the Catholic Church was not the result of a fusion of parties towards the middle of the second century, but the joint foundation of the Apostles and Prophets, Jesus Christ Himself being the Chief Corner Stone[1]— in Whom there is neither Jew nor Gentile.

[1] Ephes. ii. 20.

INDEX OF PROPER NAMES

AARON, 159.
Abraham, 158, 163.
Achaz, 72.
Adrian, Emperor, 124.
Aggeas, 162.
Agrippa, King, 133.
Alexander the Great, 57.
Anna, 164.
Andrew, St., 199.
Anicetus, Pope, 108, 109, 194-196.
Apollinaris, 196.
Apollo, 194.
Apollonius, 77, 79, 173.
Aquinas, St. Thomas—
  Faith and Reason, no opposition between, 36.
  Faith, beginning of eternal life, 37.
  God, first efficient cause, immediate action of, 28.
  Miracle, a, defined, 71; three degrees of, 72; fitting sign of Revelation, 76; does not change the plan of God's Providence but is foreseen in it, 74; the greatest miracle, the conversion of the world without a miracle, 148.
  Order of universe unchangeable as dependent on first Cause, changeable in second causes, 81, 82.
  Premovement preserves liberty, 31.
  Revelation, signs of, 32.

Salvation depends on knowledge of truth, 60.
Sin, threefold effect of, 66.
Aristeas, 77.
Aristotle, 57, 128.
Arnobius, 79.
Athanasius, St., 12.
Athenagoras, 61, 140.
Augustine, St., 11, 32, 33, 36. 39, 40, 50, 94, 109, 138, 142, 148, 168.
Augustus, Emperor, 53.

BABYLAS, 91.
Balaam, 80, 159.
Barnabas, St., 191-193.
Barnabas, 202, 203.
Basilides, 107.
Baur, Bruno, 123.
Baur, Ferdinand, 120, 144, 187, 202
Bonald, 45.
Bonnet, 87.
Bossuet, 94, 161, 169.
Buddha, 182.

CAIAPHAS, 80.
Celsus, 61, 77. 146, 172.
Cerinthius, 107, 108.
Charlemagne, 122.
Cicero, 50-53, 55, 57, 123, 153, 158, 175.
Claudius, Emperor, 99.
Clement, St., of Alexandria, 10, 106.
Clement, St., of Rome, 104, 188, 190, 193, 197, 201,

INDEX OF PROPER NAMES

Cyprian, St., 183.
Cyril, St., of Alexandria, 77.
Cyril, Bishop of Jerusalem, 167.

DANIEL, 157, 160-162.
Dante, 46, 148.
David, 159, 163.
Descartes, 56.
Deutinger, 76.
Dionysius of Corinth, 196.
Dios, 123.
Döllinger, 96.
Dryden, 90.
Du Bois Raymond, 35.
Duponceau, 46.

ELEUTHERIUS, Pope, 195, 196.
Elias, 72, 137, 143, 144.
Eliseus, 81, 137.
Elizabeth, 164.
Engelhardt, 144.
Esculapius, 79.
Eusebius, 101, 124, 195, 196.
Ezechias, 162.
Ezekiel, 49.

FICHTE, 8.

GALBA, Emperor, 53.
Gamaliel, 112.
Germanicus, 53.
Gibbon, 171.
Glaucias, 202.
Goethe, 34.
Gregory, St., the Great, 180.

HANEBERG, 107, 109, 116, 153.
Hegel, 59, 84.
Hegisippus, 107, 108, 195-197, 201.
Heine, 150.
Helmholz, 35.
Henoch, 143, 144.
Heraclitus, 50.
Herod, 123, 137, 155.
Hesiod, 50.
Hilgenfeld, 187.
Hillel, 99, 112.
Hippolytus, 197.

Holzmann, 187, 188.
Homer, 50, 123.
Horace, 58.
Humboldt, 126.
Hume, 85.

IGNATIUS, St., of Antioch, 104, 108, 194, 201.
Ignatius, St., of Loyola, 193.
Irenæus, 106, 107, 188, 190, 195, 196, 198-201.
Isaac, 159.
Isaias, 160.
Isidore, 101.

JACOB, 159.
Jacobi, 62.
James, St., 100, 189, 191, 193, 194, 201.
Jeremias, 49, 161.
Jerome, St., 101.
Jonathan, Ben Uziel, 157.
Joseph, St., 164.
Josephus, 100, 101, 123, 157, 165.
Juda, 159.
Judas, 110, 114, 165.
Julian the Apostate, Emperor, 77, 91, 136, 167.
Julian, 106.
Justin, St., 10, 42, 101, 105, 107, 169, 197, 201.

KANT, 2, 7, 8, 62.
Keim, 136, 187, 188.
Kleutgen, 1, 23.

LACTANTIUS, 173.
La Reveillière Lepeaux, 62.
Lazarus, 136.
Lessing, 84, 126.
Lives, 122, 123, 126.
Luther, 193.

MACHABEES, the, 123.
Mahomet, 181.
Malachi, 162.
Manetho, 123.
Marcion, 104, 106, 108, 109, 190, 195,

INDEX OF PROPER NAMES

Marcus Aurelius, 172.
Martha, 138.
Martial, 123.
Mary, 138.
Melchisedech, 159.
Melito, 196.
Menander, 123.
Michaelis, 116.
Micheas, 155, 160.
Minutius, Felix, 62.
Modestus, 196.
Möhler, 84.
Moleschott, 80.
Montaigne, 62.
Moses, 9, 89, 159.
Mozart, 29.
Müller, Max, 151.
Musanus, 196.

Naaman, 137.
Nahum, 49.
Nathanael, 164.
Nero, 97.
Newton, 35.
Nicodemus, 164, 174.

Onkelos, 156.
Origen, 10, 11, 79, 83.

Papias, 105, 198.
Pascal, 78, 93, 125, 154, 168, 181.
Paul, St., 5, 10, 67, 84, 91, 118, 133, 139, 140, 144, 145, 168, 172, 189-197, 200-203.
Paul, Jean, 75
Peter, St., 9, 59, 78, 114, 117, 165, 189-194, 196, 200-203.
Pfleiderer, 84.
Pheudas, 166.
Philip, St., 199.
Philip, 196.
Philo, 172.
Pinytus, 196.
Piso, 53.
Pliny, 49, 99, 124-168.
Plato, 51, 52, 56, 57, 63, 67, 90, 111, 120, 123, 126, 128, 172, 175.
Polybius, 126.

Polycarp, St., 104, 106, 108, 194, 195, 198, 200, 201.
Pomponatius, 37.
Pontius Pilate, 98, 100, 110, 140, 141, 176.
Porphery, 77.
Pothinus, Bishop of Lyons, 198.
Pourtalis, 54.
Primus, 195.
Ptolemy the Mendesian, 123.

Quadratus, 124.

Renan, 53, 58, 109, 114, 133, 136, 143, 145-147, 151, 153, 187, 188.
Rousseau, 62, 64, 83, 93, 112.
Rufinius, 101.
Ruinart, 98.

Salvador, 125.
Samuel, Rabbi, 112.
Schelling, 7, 38, 58, 121.
Schenkel, 144, 148.
Seneca, 172.
Simeon, 156, 164.
Simon Magus, 77, 78, 109, 203.
Socrates, 63, 90-99, 126, 138, 176.
Soter, Pope, 196.
Sozomen, 101.
Spinoza, 64, 80.
Staudenmeier, 42.
Steinhart, Von, 57.
Strauss, 30, 32, 80, 85, 119, 121, 136, 142-144, 148, 151, 171.
Suarez, 47.
Suetonius, 98, 158.

Tacitus, 53, 97, 98, 123, 126, 158.
Talleyrand, 62.
Tertullian, 10, 49, 100, 101, 104, 106, 107, 140, 169, 188, 190.
Theodoric, 122.
Tholuck, 46, 136.
Thucydides, 117, 123.
Tiberius, Emperor, 49, 53, 98.

Titus, St., 191.
Titus, Emperor, 166, 167.
Trajan, 99.
Trench, 79.
Trypho, 105, 197.

VAKIDI, the Pseudo, 116.
Valentinus, 107, 109.
Ventura, 45.
Vespasian, 53.
Victor, Pope, 200.

Virgil, 90, 158.
Voltaire, 121.

WISEMAN, Cardinal, 112.
Witte, De, 114.

XENOPHON, 50, 52, 67, 116, 126.

ZACHARIAS, 162, 164.
Zachary, 156.
Zeller, 86.

THE END

BURNS AND OATES, LIMITED, LONDON.

www.ingramcontent.com/pod-product-compliance
Lightning Source LLC
Chambersburg PA
CBHW021824230426
43669CB00008B/862